The Life and Career of

KLAUS BARBIE

John Beattie was born in Leeds in 1941. After attending Leeds Grammar School he enlisted in the Royal Air Force for a short period before entering journalism. He worked as a crime reporter before joining the *Sunday Express,* where he became Assistant Editor of the Manchester office. In 1980 he transferred to the *Daily Star* as Senior Feature Writer, in which capacity he has travelled the world from the North Pole to the Falkland Islands. Married with four children, he is a Wing Commander in the Royal Air Force Volunteer Reserve and lives in the Yorkshire Dales.

The Life and Career of

KLAUS BARBIE

An Eyewitness Record

JOHN BEATTIE

Methuen · London

A Methuen Paperback

First published in 1984
by Methuen London Ltd
11 New Fetter Lane, London EC4P 4EE
© 1984 Express Newspapers plc

Printed and bound in Great Britain
by Richard Clay (The Chaucer Press) Ltd
Bungay, Suffolk

ISBN 0 413 54170 3

CONTENTS

LIST OF ILLUSTRATIONS

Thanks for permission to reproduce the photographs
is due to Express Newspapers for plates
1, 2a, 2b, 2c, 3b, 4b and 8b;
to Ciaran Donnelly, *Daily Star*, for plates
3a, 4a, 6c, 7a, 7b, 7c and 8a;
and to Archives Klarsfeld for plates
5, 6a and 6b.

Author's Note

Many people have helped me during the year it has taken to research and write the story of Klaus Barbie. For some of them, their willingness to talk to me of tragic wartime events was, I know, a harrowing experience. Wounds are no less painful because they are old. To them I offer my thanks and totally inadequate sympathy. Many others gave of their time and experience to help me unravel this complex story and overcome the shortcomings of my woeful French and German. To them, I am extremely grateful. Theirs was the expertise; any errors are mine alone

Thanks, therefore, to Serge and Beate Klarsfeld, without whom no book would have been written; Ciaran Donnelly for his companionship and photography; Sue Masterman in Vienna; Edith Klebinder, Regina Sonsino, Mâitre Alain de la Servette, Arthur Thompson and Maître H. Jacubowicz in Lyon; Itta Halaunbrenner and her son Alexandre, Mary Lindell OBE and Jean-Luc Deneaux in Paris; Michael Goldberg in Versailles; René Hardy in Melle; Pierre and Monique Ardouin in Pornichet; Mike Kerrigan in Los Angeles; Fred Wehner in New York; Gottlieb Fuchs in Switzerland; David Barnouw and Eduard Groenveld of the Rijksinstituut voor Orrlogdocumentatie, Amsterdam; Henk de Ruyter of *Algemeen Dagblad*; David and Brenda Thompson in Leiden; Dik Bikker in Hilversum; Dr Josephine Butler in Durham; Philippa Kennedy and Wing Commander Mike Monks, RAF in London; Alex Dickson in Glasgow; Jill Brammer in Sheffield; Rodney S. Dalton, Fred Pawsey, Norman Tinker,

Chris Hassall and David Murdoch in Leeds; and Roger Whiteley in Pool-in-Wharfedale, for allowing me to hijack and untidy his study for a year. And to Irene Brownlee who helped immeasurably with translating and editing

J.E.B.
March 1984

PROLOGUE

It is an abiding myth that Nazi Germany was a pitiless and well-oiled machine, obediently programmed to its Führer's vision, robot-like in its single-minded efficiency. Pitiless, in a corporate sense, it certainly was. Efficient it was not. Like all dictatorships, it was smothered by a vast and complex bureaucracy, layer upon layer of it, largely unwilling to make decisions in case the wrong action should infuriate Hitler.

Nor was it particularly single-minded. Public opposition to the Führer was a thing of the past, as Captain Ernst Röhm, commander of the *Sturmabteilung* (Storm Detachment) bodyguard, had learned to his cost, along with thousands of others who were to be tortured and murdered by the SS. But opposition still existed and there were several attempts on Hitler's life, notably the bomb plot of 20 July, 1944. And when the State's systematic extermination of the Jews began, a number of SS commanders hid the Jews in their charge and blandly denied knowledge of their whereabouts to the man charged with the round-up, Adolf Eichmann.

The party leaders – Himmler, Göring, Hess, Goebbels, Ribbentrop and the rest – squabbled incessantly among themselves as they jockeyed for power and sought to find favour in the Führer's eyes. In this gang warfare there were many temporary, shaky truces in which erstwhile adversaries would join forces to discredit another faction before inevitably quarrelling and splitting yet again. The cynical and cosmopolitan citizens of the capital called this skirmishing 'the Berlin Gavotte'; it persisted, undiminished, throughout the twelve-year span of the Third Reich. The Führer, who understood better than all of them the abiding wisdom of the phrase 'divide and rule', was content to sit back in Olympian detachment and dream his own dreams of his new world.

Among the leaders, *Reichsführer* Himmler had long ago set his sights on the biggest prize of all – control of the police. But in this respect it was Hermann Göring, Minister-President of Prussia, who had made significant early gains. As a highly decorated fighter pilot (he had won the *Pour le Mérite* – the 'Blue Max' – as a member of von Richthofen's squadron on the Western Front), 'Fat Hermann' was regarded as a bluff, congenial character. In fact the overweight Göring, with his penchant for designing his own uniforms and weighing them down with medals on a scale unequalled until the advent of Idi Amin, was just as hungry for power as the rest. Prussia, because it contained Berlin, was the jewel of all the sixteen German states. As Minister-President, Göring knew that its police would form the core of a national force when the inevitable day arrived to bring all police under a unified command. The field-marshal was determined that when that day did arrive *he* would be the man in charge. To this end he dismissed almost 1,500 Prussian policemen on the grounds that they were not 'sympathetic' to the party and formed his own 'Special Duty Police Squad', in reality a personal bodyguard. Through the squad he was able to get his hands on a small, discreet but vital section of the force known as *Abteilung* IA. Though each of the sixteen state forces was autonomous, this small office in Berlin had for years played the role of a 'super Special Branch', a clearing-house for all political intelligence throughout the Reich. Under Göring's stewardship its staff was quadrupled from 60 to 250 and was gradually prised apart from the rest of the Prussian police, even to the extent of moving it to new headquarters in a disused arts and crafts school in Prinz Albrechtstrasse.

Well pleased with his work – and unaware that the

scheming Himmler would take his new toy from him almost exactly a year later – on 26 April, 1933 Göring announced a new name for the beefed-up *Abteilung* IA – *Geheime Staatspolizei* (Secret State Police).

Like many German titles it was long and unwieldly, and it was inevitable that before long a suitable and more manageable short form would be sought. This task was given to an anonymous official in the headquarters of the Berlin post office, as the title finally selected would have to be one which could be engraved easily on a franking stamp. For a couple of hours he toyed with variations of letters, scribbling them on a piece of scrap paper until he came up with a word that combined brevity with clarity of meaning. Pleased with his work in reducing the title from twenty letters to seven, he could not know that the simple acronym he had created would soon become the most sinister and dreaded word in the German language.

Gestapo!

Chapter 1

GENESIS

Anna Hees's son was born on the morning of Saturday, 25 October, 1913, in her parents' home not far from the River Rhine at Bad Godesberg, a small spa town on the fringes of Bonn, birthplace of Beethoven. The baby was not welcome. His birth brought shame to Anna and her respectable, lower-middle-class family and was a rich source of malicious gossip by the upright and outraged neighbours. For Anna, who was 27 years old, was not married, and in those pre-Great War days a single girl could commit few graver sins than to surrender her virginity and conceive a child out of wedlock. Neighbours discussed with relish the 'Hees bastard' and speculated about the identity of Anna's seducer. Herr and Frau Hees, who knew his identity, drew a crumb of comfort from the fact that he had elected to stand by their daughter and 'do the decent thing'.

On Friday, 30 January, 1914, in a church at Merzig in the Saarland, close to the French border, Anna married Nikolaus Barbie, an office clerk with aspirations of becoming a schoolteacher. Their son, by then three months old and christened Nikolaus after his father, was not present at the ceremony.

In time Herr Barbie realised his ambitions and took a step up the social ladder by securing a teaching post at an elementary school in Udler. Nikolaus junior (Klaus for short) attended the same school as a pupil, remaining there until the age of 11 when he entered Friedrich-Wilhelm High School in Trier, near Germany's border with Luxembourg.

On Saturday, 1 April, 1933, Hitler appointed Himmler to command the Bavarian police, thus setting him on the road to control of the Gestapo. On the same day 19-year-old Klaus Barbie enlisted in the Hitler Jugend, the Führer's version of the Boy Scout movement. He, like thousands of other German youths, was attracted by the comradeship, the unity of purpose and the blood-stirring rallies with their fluttering pennants and swastika flags. Best of all, after the hungry, uncertain years of Weimar, the country had a strong, hypnotic leader who preached pride when there had been only humiliation; strength and joy instead of weakness and misery.

In April the following year he graduated from high school and volunteered for a Nazi work service scheme at Neibull in Schleswig-Holstein, where he served from 26 April to 31 October. He returned to Trier to take up a voluntary post as secretary to the organiser of the party's regional headquarters.

Exactly a month before his twenty-second birthday, on 25 September, 1935, Barbie entered the service of *Reichsführer* Himmler as SS No. 272284, a keen recruit into an organisation that had become a cornerstone of the Nazi State; now its leader was in the process of fashioning it into something even greater – a State within the State.

Barbie, like every aspirant to the Order of the Death's Head, had to submit to a nine-point physical examination to satisfy SS doctors of his Nordic origins. He had also to provide a family tree dating back to 1800 to prove that there was no Jewish blood in his veins. Had he been an applicant for a commission, his proof of racial 'purity' would have had to delve back even further – to 1750. Though he was smallish – only 5 ft 6 ins – Klaus was fit and athletic. His steely grey eyes and blond hair, worn in a quiff to compensate for his lack of height, were perfect examples of the physical attributes upon which Himmler insisted – standards of selection which owed more to battery-hen farming techniques than to military recruitment or accepted anthropology.

After a probationary period he swore his oath of absolute

allegiance to Hitler, was given the rank of *Schütze* (Private) and issued with his distinctive black uniform, swastika armband, jack-boots and peaked cap with its silver skull-and-crossbones badge.

The brotherhood he had joined was an elite, fashioned by Himmler down to the very last detail and modelled on the Order of Jesuits in whose unflinching obedience to duty, coupled with matchless organisation, he saw much that he admired. Like the Jesuits the SS was governed by the strictest conditions of entry and demanded oaths of blind obedience to one man (Hitler in place of the Pope). Both conferred enormous privileges on their members.

For a long time SS members had been above the law – civil, military and party – answering only to their own courts, as Jesuit priests will submit only to the disciplines of their own Order. Party officials nicknamed Himmler 'the Black Jesuit' and even Hitler joked about 'my Ignatius Loyola'. Catholic ritual, however, had been replaced by a mystic flummery that reflected the *Reichsführer's* love of Nordic legend, feudal folklore and Teutonic romanticism.

All this Wagnerian ballyhoo, an indispensable ingredient of any SS parade or ceremonial, was cleverly blended with modern political and economic management and cold-blooded power politics into a powerful creed that reached deeply and unerringly into the German psyche. Thousands of Barbies, bewitched by it all, flocked to the crooked talisman of the swastika, and the culture that gave birth to Beethoven and Brahms spawned Belsen and Buchenwald.

When his political indoctrination and recruit training was at an end Klaus Barbie was assigned to the staff of the SD (*Sicherheitsdienst*), formed in 1932 as the Nazi Party's intelligence and security service. The job of its members was not military intelligence (that was done by the *Abwehr*, Germany's MI6), but to seek out those who by thought, word or deed were opposed to the Führer's will. At the head of the SD was the coldly handsome *Gruppenführer* (Major-General) Reinhard Heydrich, a loyal Himmler acolyte. (Heydrich was later assassinated by Czech Resistance fighters, in reprisal for which the village of Lidice, near Prague was razed and every male inhabitant murdered by the SS.)

On Saturday, 1 May 1937, Barbie joined the Nazi Party as member No. 4583085 and, the following year, was called up for national service which had been compulsory since March 1935. As a trooper in the SS, however, he was a privileged recruit, serving as a private in the 39th Infantry Regiment for a mere three months from 5 September to 3 December 1938.

Earlier that year Hitler had annexed Austria. Each concession to Hitler made him bolder and weakened the Allies' ability to resist him. There followed the Munich Agreement which dismembered Czechoslovakia, so that as Infantryman Barbie marched and drilled at the depot, his *Wehrmacht* comrades marched into the Sudetenland.

Now more than ever convinced that he could have his own way in Europe, Hitler unleashed his SS men on the Jews in what came to be known as *Kristallnacht* (plate-glass night), the systematic smashing of Jewish shops throughout Germany on the night of Wednesday, 9 November. The pogroms had begun. And, as the dark clouds of tyranny, outriders of the approaching storm of war, gathered over Europe, Barbie hung up the field-grey uniform of the *Wehrmacht* and reported for duties at SD headquarters in Dortmund, close to the heart of the industrial Ruhr.

He was quickly promoted to the rank of *Scharführer* (Staff Sergeant). With his new rank came a new girlfriend, Regina Willms, the 22-year-old daughter of a post office clerk from his adopted home-town of Trier. Born on 7 December, 1915, Regina had left high school before graduating in order to take a course in cookery and home economics. Early in 1936 she found work as a maid in Berlin before moving the following year to Düsseldorf, where she helped care for the children of party wives at a day nursery in the headquarters of the Nazi Women's Organisation. A

loyal and committed party member, No. 5429240, she
moved to Dortmund and there began steadily dating the
handsome young SS NCO whose ruthless ambition so attracted her.

On Sunday, 9 April 1939 Klaus and Regina announced
that they were officially engaged, but only after they had
gone through the catechism of regulations for love ordained
by *Reichsführer* Himmler. First they had to apply for permission from Barbie's commanding officer and submit to
him completed questionnaires drawn up by the RuSHA
(*Rasse und Siedlungshauptampt*), the SS's racial purity
board, complete with proof of Regina's Nordic origins. Then
both had to undergo medical examinations and submit
photographs of themselves dressed in swimming costumes to
show they had none of the defects of posture, skin-tone or
bone-structure that might identify them as racially inferior
types. Only when these unromantic precautions had been
taken, and it had been established beyond doubt that there
was nothing in Regina's family background that could taint
future *Herrenvolk* stock, was official blessing given to the
proposed union. Indeed, Fraülein Willm's pedigree must
have been unimpeachable, for, little more than a week after
the announcement of his engagement, Barbie was promoted
again and given the rank of *Oberscharführer* (Quarter-
master-Sergeant), one of the most senior non-commissioned
appointments in the SS.

After a year-long engagement and two weeks after
Germany invaded Denmark and Norway they were married
in Berlin on the morning of Thursday, 25 April, 1940. Even
this intensely personal moment was overshadowed by the
ideological mystique dictated by Himmler for such cere-
monies. It was forbidden for SS men to attend church and
no priest was allowed at their weddings, deathbeds or their
children's christenings. So the couple went through a short
civil ceremony, attended only by immediate family, at the
Berlin Register Office. Then followed a marriage vow ritual
conducted at HQ by the local SS commander. The witnesses

were two SS comrades, *Obersturmführer* (Lieutenant) Eric Goebel and Paul Neukirchen. Among the wedding presents were the standard, symbolic SS gifts to newly-weds – bread and salt.

For the couple the occasion was a double celebration, for only five days earlier Barbie had received notification of his commissioning as *Untersturmführer* (Second Lieutenant) in the 'Superior Service'. There was just enough warning for him to get a smart new officer's uniform and soft leather jack-boots for the big day.

The recommendation for his commission (a leap of three ranks) read: '*Oberscharführer* Barbie is an irreproachable comrade. His service achievements are excellent. His attitude to the SS, both on and off duty, is impeccable.' His attitude to life, it said, was 'firm'.

Untersturmführer and Frau Barbie moved into furnished rooms in 28 Horstwesselstrasse (named after a Nazi 'martyr'), not far from the SS HQ in Dortmund. But within a month of the wedding a posting notice dropped through the letter box, sent from the head office of the Gestapo in Berlin's Prinz Albrechtstrasse. He was to report for duty in Holland.

On 10 May, flushed with his previous month's conquests in Norway and Denmark, Hitler unleashed his armies on France, Holland and Belgium. The attack could have been straight out of the manual of the new art of warfare so aptly named *Blitzkrieg*. The small Belgian Army and that of France – supposedly Europe's greatest – collapsed in disarray under the onslaught. The Dutch Army, however, fought fiercely in the flat, open countryside, stubbornly extracting a heavy price for every mile of the *Wehrmacht's* advance.

It took Hermann Göring, the fat field-marshal and commander-in-chief of the Luftwaffe, to bring the Netherlanders to their knees. He dispatched massive formations of bombers over Rotterdam and within hours the city was a mass of flames. The constant carpet bombing killed thousands of men, women and children and reduced the port's inner city to a heap of smouldering rubble. Then he sent an ultimatum to the Dutch Army commander, General Winkelman: unless his forces capitulated immediately and unconditionally further Heinkels and Junkers would be launched on The Hague, Amsterdam, Utrecht and Haarlem. Winkelman had no choice. And so, on 15 May, with bands braying triumphantly, the German Army marched in as conquerors.

Close on their heels, like a shadowy and sinister band of camp followers, came the Gestapo.

On Saturday, 25 May, Barbie arrived in the capital, The Hague, to take up his new appointment as an intelligence officer in the SD's Bureau for Jewish Affairs, but was soon detached for duties in Gestapo HQ in Euterpestraat (now Van der Veen Straat) amid the maze of canals that is Amsterdam. There he hung up his uniform for most of the time, favouring the trench coat and trilby hat that was the civilian 'uniform' of the Gestapo, and flung himself zealously into his new task as a member of an *Einsatzkommando* (Action Group).

These mobile hit squads, a brainchild of Heydrich, existed to follow the *Wehrmacht* into occupied territories to mop up enemies, real or imagined, of the Reich. These included Jews who had fled Germany to escape the pogroms (and later all Jews), Resistance leaders, trade-unionists, Communists, gypsies and Freemasons.

The *modus operandi* of the *Einsatzkommandos* was direct, brutal and effective. A victim would be selected and two or three car-loads of Gestapo operatives, flanked by SS motor-cycle troops, dispatched to arrest him, usually in the early hours of the morning. Before moving in, gas supplies to the victim's house or flat would be disconnected, for the Gestapo had more than once been robbed of a prey who had gassed himself in the oven rather than face torture and lingering death. The building would be surrounded so that every possible escape route was blocked.

Then would come the knock on the door. If the response was slow it would be kicked in and the suspect dragged from his bed while SS men held back his wife and children. He would be manhandled into the street and bundled into one of the waiting cars. What happened next usually depended on the suspect's offence.

Jews and other fugitives from the Führer's 'justice' were merely taken to cells and held there pending transfer to a concentration camp; others were frequently shot out of hand in some lonely spot and flung into a shallow grave. But the most wretched were Resistance workers, Allied agents or others who possessed information wanted by the Germans. For them the most unspeakable tortures lay in store as guards at Gestapo HQ were let loose on them with orders to make them talk.

Those who were allowed to live were arraigned before no court; faced no formal charge; had no legal representation. Some, indeed, were totally mystified by their arrest, for the Gestapo, for all its reputation for murderous efficiency, could be incredibly slipshod and sometimes picked up totally blameless citizens. More than one victim died in bewilderment amid the squalid horror of a concentration camp for no better reason than that he shared the same – or similar – name as a wanted man.

Those who were slaughtered out of hand often simply vanished for ever, their bodies disposed of by burial or cremation while their distraught relations frantically and fruitlessly sought news of them from the authorities. In some instances the remains were returned to horrified families who would be presented with a box of ashes or a sealed coffin which they were warned not to open.

Like all dictators, be they of the right or left, Hitler was paranoid, constantly imagining plots and conspiracies against himself. The war which he himself had unleashed on the world was, he believed, the result of a giant international conspiracy by Zionists, Jewish financiers, Marxists and Freemasons.

Among this uneasy collection of imagined bedfellows, the Führer reserved a special hatred for Freemasons. Their international bonds, combining religion and charity with a dedication to upholding the fabric of society, overlaid with ritual and secrecy, were seen by Hitler as a threat to his grip on his subjects. From the earliest days of the Third Reich members of Masonic orders were persecuted ruthlessly.

In Amsterdam Barbie was given the task of translating this fear of Freemasonry into direct action; leaders of the craft were ordered to disband their lodges and seal up the temples. They obeyed Barbie's edicts but braver souls among them continued to practise by holding clandestine meetings in hotels, business premises or members' homes.

Hermannus van Tongeren, a 64-year-old Amsterdam businessman, was Grand Master of Holland's National Order of Freemasons, but what should have been the highlight of his masonic career became instead a time of bitter disappointment as he presided over the dismantling of the Order. On Thursday, 10 October 1940, he received a telephone call from a highly distressed friend telling him that six brother masons, preparing for a secret lodge meeting in the Hotel Americain, had been arrested by the Gestapo.

Knowing that other masons were on their way to the makeshift lodge and would walk into the trap, he courageously ignored the fact that he was a marked man and hurried round to the hotel entrance in Leidseplein to intercept others heading for the meeting.

'Gestapo!' he hissed as each arrived. 'Keep walking. Warn any of the others you might see.' By this means he managed to prevent any other lodge members from walking into Barbie's ambush – but only at a terrible cost to himself. Van Tongeren suspected that the young *Untersturmführer* might have a plain-clothes man posted outside the hotel and this, indeed, was the case; when eventually the *Einsatzkommando* returned to HQ the old man's presence in Leidseplein was reported to Barbie.

'Next day three SS officers came to our house in a *Wehr-macht* car and demanded to know where my father was,' Charlotta van Tongeren, 81 years old and living in an old people's home, recalled in March 1983. She continued:

I was terrified but managed to lie by saying he was at the hairdresser's. They said: "OK, get in the car and show us the way."

I directed them to a nearby hairdresser's, but of course my father wasn't there. We all got back in the car and drove round for a time while I pretended to be looking for another shop where he might be. I chose one at random, but naturally they drew a blank there, too. They began to get angry. They shoved me back into the car and we drove back to our house.

By the most appalling stroke of bad luck we pulled up just as my father was letting himself into the front door. I was thrown out of the car, my father was bundled into it and driven off at high speed. The whole family was beside itself with anxiety because we had no idea where my father had been taken or what would happen to him. We began to fear we would never see him again.

That evening a friend of my father's called – Johan de Vries, who was a member of the International League of Freemasons. He told us he'd managed to follow the Gestapo men and discover where my father was being held and that we would be able to visit him once a fortnight. He'd even learned the names of the arresting officers – Kempin, Kalb and Barbie.

Each time we visited my father we had to get a permit from the SS offices in the centre of Amsterdam, close to the Dam, from the very men who had arrested him. Kempin and Kalb used to man the counter to deal with enquiries from the public. Barbie, being the boss, used to sit at the back of the office. Every time I saw him he was listening to loud music from a radio on his desk. He was always cracking jokes and the other two used to roar with laughter; I suppose they thought it best to humour the boss.

When we visited my father he leaned very close to me and whispered: 'Watch out for the one called Barbie, who sometimes uses the name Weber ... he's the most dangerous one of them all.'

For five months van Tongeren was Barbie's prisoner in Amsterdam, five months when he was half starved and kept short of drinking water which he needed for a painful and debilitating kidney complaint. In March 1941, shaking with fever, he was herded into a crowded open cattle truck at the start of a five-day rail journey to Sachsenhausen concentration camp. Within a week of his arrival he was dead.

On Tuesday, 1 April, the van Tongeren family received a telephone call from Klaus Barbie, preremptorily ordering them to report to his office near the Dam. There, without preamble or any expression of regret, he told 39-year-old Charlotta: 'Your father is dead. He had a double ear infection. His body has already been cremated.' A week later his ashes were delivered to the house.

Watch out for the one called Barbie, the old man had warned. His grieving family could not know that three years later they would hear the name again and that once more its owner would plunder them of a loved one. . . .

Van Tongeren's arrest and transportation was something of a coup for Barbie and within five weeks of the arrest he was promoted to the rank of *Obersturmführer* (Lieutenant). The gazetting of that promotion – dated Saturday, 9 November, 1940 – was backed by a senior officer's confidential report which noted that Barbie was 'a diligent and sound colleague' who possessed intellect 'in good measure'. His strength of will was 'pronounced', his judgement 'firm and clear' and his appearance and conduct 'disciplined and impeccable'. He was, the report concluded, 'zestful, truthful and friendly'.

Except for this 'friendly' officer and the excesses of his *Einsatzkommando* (and others elsewhere in Holland), the German occupation was, in its early stages, a model of correctness. Hitler was anxious that Germany's Dutch 'cousins', with their origins in Saxony and their shared language roots, should be allowed to live their lives with the minimum of interference. The SS aside, ordinary *Wehrmacht* soldiers were under the strictest instructions to be polite and helpful to the local populace.

'We have not come here to threaten or destroy a culture or to deprive a country of its freedom,' the new Nazi Governor, Arthur Seyss-Inquart, said in a broadcast to the Dutch people.

Such speeches, backed by the punctilious behaviour of the rank and file of the German Army, did much to reassure many Dutch people that the Nazis were not the ogres they had been led to believe. There was a significant upsurge in recruitment to Anton Mussert's Dutch Nazi Party (the NSB), though their would-be storm-troopers were astounded when the Germans banned their newspaper *De Doodsklok* (The Clock of Death) because it was judged to be too virulently anti-Semitic! Some NSB members actually joined the Waffen-SS, the fully militarized fighting arm of the SS, and fought with these crack units on the Russian front later in the war.

For the majority of the Dutch, however, the honeymoon period was short-lived. By early 1941 Barbie and his colleagues were assiduously compiling lists of Jews from public records and had sent an order to all café owners forbidding them to serve Jews with food or drink. Those who were slow to comply lost their windows – smashed by SS troopers using as missiles that most common of Dutch commodities, bicycles.

At this time, Berlin was the breeding ground of a slowly forming master plan that was so hideous that even hardened Nazis could barely believe it ... the so-called 'Final Solution' to the Jewish 'problem'. Conceived by Hitler and his Propaganda Minister Josef Goebbels, abetted by Göring, this was the planned, systematic extermination of European Jewry. Even Himmler seemed to view the coming genocide with foreboding, confiding in his masseur, Felix Kersten: 'I never wanted to destroy the Jews. I had quite different ideas, but now Goebbels has it all on his conscience.'

Himmler's scruples, if he had them, were short-lived, overshadowed by his slavish obedience to the Führer's will, and he threw himself into the task of overlording what was to become the most grisly episode of modern times.

He selected the trusted Heydrich to create the vast organisation that would be necessary and appointed *Ober-sturmbannführer* (Lieutenant-Colonel) Adolf Eichmann to take charge of Gestapo Desk IV B 4 in a confiscated masonic lodge at 116 Kurfürstenstrasse, Berlin. From there he wrestled with the complex logistical problem of tracking down millions of Jews and transporting them to the death camps. Eichmann − later kidnapped, tried and executed by the Israelis − was the spider at the centre of a web whose threads stretched across an entire continent.

As he formulated his transport plans, one of his minions, Barbie, was concerning himself with personal problems. Regina was pregnant and, alone in the house in Dortmund, was not having an easy time. Her pregnancy was a difficult one, made worse by the constant RAF bombing raids on the city. Some time in the spring of 1941 she packed up her belongings and moved south to live with her mother at 5 Liebfrauenstrasse, Trier.

There, on Monday, 30 June, after a difficult and painful delivery, she gave birth to a daughter. The fair-haired child was christened Ute, but − as had been the case at her parents' wedding − no priest was allowed to attend the christening. In place of baptism there was an SS ceremony at which were handed over the gifts ordained by Himmler as suitable for first-born children of his Order − a silver beaker and spoon and a blue silk shawl, produced at the SS-owned factory at Allach, near Munich.

Eight days before her birth Hitler had astounded the world by diverting troops from the west, so postponing the planned invasion of Britain, to open up a new front in the east against his ertswhile allies, the Russians.

As the jubilant *Wehrmacht* drove back the ill-equipped Red Army they were at first cheered and welcomed as liberators by the Russian people, who saw the chance to shrug off the yoke of Communist oppression that had gripped them for more than two decades. But the euphoria did not last long. With the *Wehrmacht's* rear echelons came the *Einsatzkommandos* who proved themselves to be every bit as murderous and merciless as Stalin's version of the Gestapo, the NKVD (today known as the KGB). They lost no time in establishing a reign of terror: thousands of real or imagined 'enemies of the Reich' were rounded up to be machine-gunned, hanged from trees or lampposts or transported to concentration camps. With them into forced labour and the gas ovens went 900,000 Russian Jews, doomed to death like the 3,000,000 from Poland (90 per cent of the country's Jewish population) whose round-up had begun in September 1939.

Inevitably the Final Solution juggernaut turned westwards to Holland where Barbie and his men had been tabulating the whereabouts of every known Jew in Amsterdam. By May 1942 the first of Eichmann's deportation trains had begun to roll into the city's railway sidings and thousands of men, women and children were crammed into wagons for the nightmare one-way journey.

Many had been sold to the Nazis by their neighbours, for the Nazis paid a bounty of 7.50 guilders (about £1.75 at 1983 exchange rates) for each Jew. But many, many more were caught because of the painstaking work of *Obersturmführer* Klaus Barbie.

By then, however, rewarded with an Iron Cross (Second Class) and his work in the city of Rembrandt ended for the time being, he had moved on.

To France.

Chapter 2

BETRAYAL

What Kaiser Wilhelm and General Ludendorff had failed to do in four years, former Corporal Hitler and General Heinz Guderian were to achieve in four weeks in 1940.

Spearheaded by armoured units racing over ground already softened by the Luftwaffe, the German Army bored through Belgium with almost contemptuous ease, gaining ground fast and mopping up resistance in its wake. The British Northern Army and the French Seventh Army advanced to help the beleaguered Belgians, the French moving so hastily that they outstripped their ammunition supply lines.

Neither army proved to be much more than an irritant to General Guderian who neatly side-stepped them by swerving to the south and, with his XIX Panzer Corps, reached the River Meuse on 12 May. The following day General Erwin Rommel's 7th Panzer Division crossed the Meuse at Huy while Guderian established bridgeheads at Sedan, over-powering two French divisions which fell back in panic. By 15 May, ten Panzer divisions had bulldozed through the Ardennes to take Laon and Saint-Quentin, sixty miles inside France.

French military philosophy, which had advanced little since the huge static battles of the Great War, had based the security of France on the 'impregnable' Maginot Line. But the miles of underground fortresses and gun emplacements proved to be one of the costliest follies of the century for the German Army merely weaved and passed them by.

On 16 May, six days after becoming Britain's Prime Minister on the resignation of Neville Chamberlain, Winston

Churchill flew to Paris for an emergency meeting with Paul Reynaud. Churchill was determined to stiffen the backbone of the French premier who had the day before wailed to him on the telephone: 'We have been defeated – we have lost the battle!'

Churchill was horrified by the meeting. In his *Second World War* he wrote: 'Utter dejection was on every face.' He asked the whereabouts of the strategic reserve and was stunned when a general shook his head, shrugged his shoulders and replied: 'There is none.'

'What were we to think of the great French Army and its highest chiefs?' he wrote. 'It had never occurred to me that any commanders having to defend 500 miles of engaged front would have left themselves unprovided with a mass of manoeuvre.'

Misplaced faith in the Maginot Line had meant that the French simply had no troops in reserve. Angered and shaken by France's folly, Churchill returned to London and gave the orders for the British Expeditionary Force to withdraw from its advanced but untenable positions. Had the French been able to make a real counter-attack, the British would have remained. Now Churchill was determined that the incompetence of the French High Command was not going to be paid for with the blood of the BEF. Fighting spiritedly they retreated towards the Channel ports.

Many French *poilus* fought stubbornly alongside them on the long and demoralising retreat that was to lead to a small seaside town called Dunkirk, and individual French units, notably those at Laon and Abbeville, made gallant counter-attacks against the Germans. But the French Army as a whole proved to be a busted flush. Order, counter-order, disorder – the old military adage had never proved to be more true than it was in May 1940. The roads of north-eastern France were choked not only with terrified refugees but with leaderless French soldiers fleeing the battle. There were many ugly scenes as the defenders of France commandeered cars and lorries from their owners at gunpoint.

The retreat turned into a rout. Ditches and hedgerows were littered with abandoned weapons and uniforms; gun emplacements which should have bombarded the advancing Germans remained silent, deserted by their crews. In places officers tried to stem the tide but were ignored by their soldiers. Many joined the deserters who were throwing off their uniforms and heading for home. Thousands surrendered and tailed miserably along in the wake of the victorious *Wehrmacht*.

It was, with a few gallant exceptions, a total shambles. The Fall of France quickly turned into what must rank as the greatest débâcle of twentieth-century warfare.

On Friday, 14 June, Paris was declared an open city and the German Army marched in past the Arc de Triomphe. Two days later Britain, in desperation, offered France a union of the two empires to fuse the two nations into one to continue the fight against Nazism. But that day Reynaud resigned as premier and proposed as his successor Marshal Philippe Pétain who, within twenty-four hours, was suing for peace.

On Friday, 21 June, France signed the surrender document at Compiègne – in the very same railway carriage in which the Germans had surrendered twenty-two years earlier. Hitler was present to witness the sweet revenge and could not resist a jack-booted dance of triumph as he made his way towards the carriage entrance.

A shameful defeat was soon to be followed by an equally shameful Occupation. . . .

Vichy is a small and elegant spa town north-west of Lyon, famous for its natural mineral waters, and – from 1940 to 1944 – infamous as the seat of France's collaborationist government under the leadership of Marshal Pétain, the 'Victor of Verdun'.

In this, France's hour of trial, 'Père' Pétain, who had been largely responsible for the woeful inadequacies of the Maginot Line, was a far from convincing leader. Approaching senility had robbed him of any decisiveness he might once have boasted, though many recalled that even in 1917 – the year of his greatest glory – he had been known as something of a defeatist. Premier Georges Clemenceau had said that he 'had to kick Pétain into victory up the backside'.

The 84-year-old Marshal was an ultra-right-wing conservative and shared many of Hitler's views on the future of Europe and the dangers it faced from the spread of Communism. With few qualms and little demur, the ageing war-horse set about the task of delivering his homeland into the hands of the Nazis; the arch-collaborator in charge of a country whose citizens, four decades on, are still haunted by the spectre of their own collaboration.

The new President of France installed himself in Vichy's best hotel, the Hôtel du Parc, and his hastily formed cabinet requisitioned other hotels as their ministerial offices. There was hopeless overcrowding and a lot of undignified rank-pulling as ministers sought to secure for themselves the most prestigious accommodation. Junior ministers and civil servants had to make do with poky closets and, in some cases, bathrooms.

When the scramble was over France had become two countries. Occupied France in the north, two-thirds of the nation, was under the direct control of the German High Command; the remainder was administered by the Vichy government. The armistice demanded that all French forces be disarmed and their weapons handed over; that any Germans – mainly anti-Nazi refugees – should be returned to the Fatherland; and that France should pay the maintenance costs of the occupying troops, thus financing her own bondage.

Vichy officials worked with a will to impose these conditions on their fellow-countrymen, proclaiming a 'national revolution' to purge the country of its decadent liberalism under the watchwords *Travail, Famille, Patrie* (Work, Family, Country). The disillusioned French quickly made up their own version – *Trahison, Famine, Prisons*

(Treason, Famine, Prisons).

Within Pétain's slogan lay the germ of a reactionary philosophy that was to lead to the extermination of almost 70,000 Jews, transported to Hitler's gas ovens during the four-year span of Vichy rule — *not*, as some still believe, because the French were coerced into obeying the orders of their German masters but because it was *official policy* as decreed by Pétain and his government. Many Jews were rounded up by Barbie and others like him, but with less than 2,500 operatives scattered throughout France the Gestapo and SD were grossly overworked. So many more were arrested by fellow Frenchmen wearing the familiar blue képi of the *gendarmerie*. Though sometimes they were less brutal than their German opposite numbers (but not always), it made no difference in the end to those arrested who still faced the same internment in holding camps and eventual transportation to Auschwitz or other extermination camps.

The roots of anti-Semitism in Europe go back many centuries, during which France was blighted by its fair share of pogroms, but by the 1930s a new liberalism and tolerance had grown in the country. By then the Third Republic was recognised as a haven for thousands of religious and political refugees who had fled from Hitler's Germany, Stalin's Russia, Mussolini's Italy and Franco's Spain.

This new cosmopolitan France was not, however, universally welcomed. There were those in France who sought to stir deep fears with talk of 'loss of national identity' and 'racial impurities'. It was the same tub that Hitler, Mussolini, Moseley and dozens of other would-be Fascist leaders throughout Europe had thumped for years. As the influx of refugees grew bigger throughout the thirties, so the siren message of the anti-Semites found increasingly sympathetic ears.

By 1939 the refugee problem was costing France 200 million francs a month and, with war looming, a series of emergency measures was introduced which led to the rounding up and internment of foreign nationals in *camps de concentration.* Those who were found to be politically harmless were released, only to be reinterned during the chaos of the invasion by harassed officials who could think of nothing better to do with them.

When Vichy was born 40,000 civilians – around 70 per cent of them Jewish – were already interned in Unoccupied France, ready-made hostages to fortune. To their number were added thousands of Jews expelled by the Germans from Occupied France. In those days, before the advent of the 'Final Solution', the Nazis were only too pleased to rid themselves of the Jews by foisting them on to Vichy.

As French officials were swamped by the sheer magnitude of the task, their methods – inevitably – became harsher and more arbitrary. Unable to cope with each individual's unique problems, they quickly resorted to playing the numbers' game. So it was that families were torn apart, fathers going to one camp, mothers to another, children to yet a third. Food and water were in short supply, medical care inadequate and living conditions primitive.

Some German Jews who had fled from the Nazis to France before the war became so exhausted and desperate they even turned to Germany for help. A group of Jewish ex-servicemen, veterans of the Kaiser's army, appealed to the Foreign Office in Berlin for aid against the 'inhuman conditions . . . too bad for black slaves' of the French camp at Saint-Cyprien.

'Here we are,' they wrote, 'Germans first, before anything else, and forevermore Germans.' Their treatment, they claimed, was an insult to Germany and, as former German soldiers, they sought the protection of the Reich. One can only wonder at the reaction of Foreign Minister von Ribbentrop to such an ingenuous plea. . . .

On 27 August Vichy repealed the Marchandeau Law, an executive order of April 1939 which had amended the Press Law of 1881 by outlawing any newspaper attack 'toward a group of persons who belong by origin to a particular race or religion when it is intended to arouse hatred among citizens or residents'.

Worse was to follow. On 30 October, 1940 the *Statut des Juifs* (Statute on the Jews) was introduced, a document that was chillingly reminiscent of many of the anti-Semitic edicts that had emanated from Himmler's desk in Berlin. It began by defining those who, in the eyes of the French State, were Jewish and then barring them from all positions of importance in the public service, the officer corps and NCO ranks, and from any opinion-shaping profession: teaching, journalism, and work in radio, film and theatre. Other legislation set up a commission to review all naturalisations granted since 1927, as a result of which more than 15,000 French citizens – among them 6,000 Jews – were quite arbitrarily stripped of their nationality. A law of 4 October, 'concerning foreigners of the Jewish race' authorised prefects (powerful local representatives – almost governors – of central government) to intern foreign Jews in 'special camps' or to force them to live under police surveillance in remote rural communities.

For more than four decades thousands of Frenchmen have taken some comfort from the belief that such shameful laws were forced on an unwilling France by her German conquerors; that the captive State could do little but bow to Nazi demands for action against the Jews. Such comfort is ill-founded. The myth was destroyed, in fact, soon after the end of the war, but many in France have chosen to continue to believe it. Perhaps the last service – indeed the only service – that Klaus Barbie can give France is to spotlight the truth and make her citizens face it squarely.

The author of the notorious *Statut des Juifs* was Raphael Alibert, Pétain's Minister of Justice, who along with other high-ranking collaborators was brought to trial after the liberation. During the proceedings the attorney-general was astonished to discover that Alibert's dossier contained not a single atom of evidence of any contact, official or unofficial, with the Germans regarding anti-Jewish measures. Ironically because of this the State was obliged to drop the charge that Alibert dealt with the enemy. Every comma of the infamous statute was home-grown, French-inspired to the last letter. Nor has any historian come up since that trial with a single document emanating in 1940 from the Germans ordering the Vichy government to introduce anti-Semitic legislation.

The occupying German Army had, in any case, far too many other worries to bother themselves overmuch by rounding up Jews for Himmler, for whom most professional *Wehrmacht* officers had a deep dislike and mistrust. Despite their best efforts to smash the remnants of the BEF, they had been forced to witness the successful evacuation from Dunkirk of 338,226 Allied soldiers – 26,000 of them French – aboard a motley collection of ships and small boats in June.

Now in the process of being rearmed and re-equipped, those Dunkirk veterans would be a valuable addition to the British Army, a formidable counter to the German troops massing in France for the final push across the Channel into western Europe's last fortress against Nazidom. The invasion barges were ready in the Channel ports; nothing, it appeared, could stop the Germans from conquering Britain.

So that his invasion fleet might cross the Channel unmolested, Hitler ordered Göring to destroy the Royal Air Force and so remove the final obstacle to 'Operation Sealion'. All through that blazing summer of 1940 the Luftwaffe sought to clear the skies of the RAF in what was to become enshrined in British history as the Battle of Britain. In the end, though, it was the Spitfires and Hurricanes which won and gave Hitler his first bloody nose of the war.

But as long as the battle raged and Operation Sealion was 'on' the German commanders could ill-afford to waste time chasing Jews. Those they did find they usually bundled across the demarcation line into Unoccupied France, only too pleased to rid themselves of some of the appalling refugee problems that beset them.

Affronted Vichy officials would often shunt them back north and try to sneak them back into the Occupied Zone. In these macabre games of shuttlecock the sufferers were locked up in carriages and trucks; some trains reached their eventual destination with a corpse or two jammed in amongst the horrified and demoralised passengers. There were even cases of refugees being put aboard scheduled passenger trains by the Germans, given tickets, false papers and a packet of sandwiches, and told to bluff their way into Vichy France. In the belief that they would fare better there most were only too willing to play their part in the charade ... though most were quickly disillusioned when they discovered that their treatment by their fellow-countrymen was no better, and sometimes worse, than they had received at the hands of the Germans.

Pamphlets circulated by Pétain's propaganda department sought to justify the regime's anti-Semitism on the grounds of 'defence of the race, the family, youth and the professions'. After all, explained one leaflet, Jews who had rendered exceptional service to their country or who had won military honours were exempted from the restrictions placed on their co-religionists: 'They prove that it has never entered into Marshal Pétain's intentions to penalise for their origins men who ... have enhanced French prestige.' By means of this hypocritical and selective persecution, two army officers – General Darius-Paul Bloch and Chief of Artillery Squadron Pierre Brissac – were permitted to keep their commissions. Ten university professors were allowed to retain their chairs and some scientists were able to hang on to their higher civil service posts.

As a result of the favourable treatment meted out to old soldiers, a quiet backwater of the War Ministry – the Committee for Review of Military Decorations – suddenly found itself projected into the arena of politics as it became inundated with querulous memos from the Commission for Jewish Affairs. For a Jewish ex-serviceman the award of a sufficiently prestigious medal or honour could mean the difference between keeping a job or being thrown out of work. Later it was to mean the difference between life and death.

The Commissioner-General for Jewish Affairs, Xavier Vallat, began bombarding the committee with demands for quick decisions about Jews who had been recommended for decorations during the invasion. Until the awards were confirmed or turned down, he claimed, their cases could not be settled. In a letter to the committee he warned: '. . . when the recipient is a Jew, I call your attention to the grave consequences of approving them too easily or too liberally.' The War Ministry was notoriously harsh in its application of anti-Jewish laws, having gone one stage beyond the government ban on Jewish officers and NCOs by even barring Jews from the ranks and then issuing a recruiting poster guaranteeing that volunteers would not have to associate with Jews.

The committee was incensed by the zealous commissioner-general's attempts to instruct it in its duties and wrote back frostily: 'To accomplish its difficult task, the committee has the absolute moral duty to bring total impartiality to its judgements. Jews have neither benefited from any indulgence whatsoever nor been treated with exceptional severity.' In this one case a small civil service department had behaved honourably and confounded Vallat by scrupulously insisting on treating Jews like every other French citizen.

This was a rare exception. As Jews became increasingly harassed, stripped first of their dignity, later of their possessions and finally of their loved ones, to be herded into hastily constructed internment camps, fewer and fewer voices were raised on their behalf.

Many strove to escape from Hitler's Europe, which they sensed would soon become their killing ground, but a largely indifferent world ignored their plight. Their nearest bolt-hole, Switzerland, sealed her borders and turned back Jews who clamoured for asylum. The United States reduced her flow of entry visas to a mere trickle once the elite of scientists, teachers, doctors and others had been creamed off. Spain and Portugal began refusing transit visas which had once been freely granted. The British government declined to take any more refugees, claiming that to do so would inflame anti-Semitism in cities which had only recently witnessed the racial violence whipped up by Sir Oswald Moseley's Fascist blackshirts. At the same time Whitehall slammed shut the gates of Palestine, the homeland for which Jews yearned. The mandarins of the Foreign Office predicted that any further influx of Jews would inevitably damage already strained Anglo-Arab relations.

As the world turned its back on European Jewry Hitler turned his back on logic and the still-unconquered British Isles. To the astonishment of the world he invaded Russia in June 1941. Operation Sealion was shelved indefinitely as the Führer flung three million men, 3,580 tanks and 1,830 aircraft into a 1,800-mile front in an effort to lay waste Stalin's Communist empire. But when, after the first spectacular gains of the *Blitzkrieg*, that campaign lurched to a halt as the Red Army dug in, Hitler became frustrated. Bogged down in the east and west, he began to brood about other matters – even more hideous than total war. . . .

Incarcerated with the Jews in Fortress Europe, unable to boot them out of Germany or any of the Occupied territories and with the war now static for the first time, Hitler was faced with the prospect of either shelving the Jewish problem until the end of an ever-lengthening war or seeking a drastic solution immediately.

That solution – the Final Solution – emerged at a meeting of Nazi warlords held on Tuesday, 20 January, 1942, at 56–8 Am Grossen Wannsee, Berlin, convened by Heydrich, Himmler's deputy. Adolf Eichmann, by then head of the Jewish section within the Reich Central Security Department, (RSHA) took the minutes. That such a relatively senior officer (a lieutenant-colonel) should act as secretary demonstrates the secrecy of the meeting. Only thirty copies of the minutes were made and those which survive make chilling reading.

Heydrich spoke of huge labour columns undergoing hardships which would lead to the 'natural decline' of all but the very strongest, with special treatment — unspecified — for those who managed to survive the 'process of natural selection'. He added that practical experience, of major importance to 'the final solution of the Jewish question', was even then being gathered. What he meant was the murderous activities of the *Einsatzkommandos* and *Einsatzgruppen* who had swept into Russia in the wake of the fighting soldiers to begin the systematic extermination of Jews, Communists, and other enemies of the Reich. They had made a start by machine-gunning and hanging, but both methods were tedious and time-wasting; now the SS men were fast learning more efficient techniques of mass slaughter.

One, pioneered by an SS officer called Walter Rauff, involved the diverting of a truck's exhaust gases into the rear passenger compartment. It proved to be popular for three reasons: it was cheap, costing not a penny more than the normal transport costs; it was efficient — no one survived the carbon monoxide poisoning and the bodies were ready for immediate disposal at the end of the delivery run; finally it was easier for the overworked murder squads and not as upsetting to those few SS men who might have scruples left about shooting victims who were often women and children. Rauff's neat and cost-effective scheme so delighted his masters, who never had to listen to the pounding of fists on the van walls as the victims began to choke, or hear the terrified screaming of children as they clung to parents who were powerless to help them, that they used it as a basis for the bigger, permanent gas chambers soon to be built at the death camps.

Until his death in May 1984, Walter Rauff lived in Chile, where he maintained his interest in butchery by running a meat-freezing plant.

As the meeting progressed, Heydrich revealed the breathtaking magnitude of his assignment – no less than a sweep of Europe from west to east to round up every Jewish man, woman and child, including – after the eventual invasion of Britain – those who lived in London, Manchester, Leeds and all the other traditional concentrations of British Jewry. Eleven million people in all . . . a whole race, culture and religion to be wiped off the face of the globe. No wonder there were only thirty copies of the minutes. . . .

Within weeks of that meeting there began a wide-ranging series of personnel changes among the top German and French officials concerned with the fate of France's Jews. By May Xavier Vallat, who was anti-Semitic but didn't like the Germans and wanted to persecute his country's Jews without meddling by outsiders, was replaced as Commissioner-General for Jewish Affairs. His successor was Louis Darquier, a one-time agitator who was even more virulently anti-Semitic than Vallat, fond of thumping Jews in public and only too pleased to pander to the Germans. Darquier enthusiastically supported German decrees which demanded that every Jew should wear a Star of David (for which the individual had to use his own precious clothing coupons) on his coat, even though his Vichy masters were against the idea and never implemented it. The Germans went ahead anyway in the Occupied Zone but discovered to their chagrin that the star was counter-productive. This, the first outward sign of segregation, was seen by many Frenchmen as an affront to human dignity. Parisian Gentiles began giving up their seats on the Métro to those wearing the star; there was mounting public nausea as Frenchmen for the first time, began to recognise the true face of Nazism.

Out of office, too, went the German Supreme Commander in France, General Otto von Stülpnagel, an officer of the old school, who demonstrated his repugnance to the SS's reprisal executions by resigning. He was replaced by his cousin, General Karl Heinrich von Stülpnagel, who promptly issued a circular citing Hitler's latest order: for every killing of a German, not only would hostages be executed but 500 Jews and Communists would be deported to the east. Reserves of hostages would be interned at a camp at Compiègne to be drawn upon as necessary.

Most ominous of all the changes was the removal from the German High Command in Paris of responsibility for police operations. The new head of police was SS-*Gruppenführer* Carl Oberg, answerable only to Himmler in Berlin. And Himmler was answerable only to Hitler.

So, with a few deft changes of policy and personnel, a 42-year-old Bavarian chicken farmer cleared the boards and prepared to murder the Jews of France.

On Thursday, 21 May, Klaus Barbie took up a new appointment as head of the *Einsatzkommando* in the small and picturesque town of Gex, north of Geneva and close to France's border with Switzerland. His posting there was part of Oberg's 'new broom' policy for policing France, for the young *Obersturmführer* was just the sort of operative he wanted – youthful, zealous and efficient. When the day came, as come it soon would, for the mass deportations to the killing factories in the east, men like Barbie would be invaluable.

His job in Gex was to comb the surrounding countryside for Jews and others who might try to flee the coming holocaust by illegally crossing into neutral Switzerland. The fact was, though, that few managed the journey – not so much through Barbie's labours but because of the effectiveness with which the Swiss had sealed their borders. A high proportion of those who did contrive to smuggle themselves into the country were promptly escorted to the frontier and bundled back into France. Switzerland, the traditionally neutral lamb, was not about to offend Hitler, the wolf, and give him an excuse to overrun this tiny oasis of peace in the heart of a war.

Of Barbie's six-month posting to Gex little is known. Nowhere in the town could I find anyone who remembered the man. Though everyone, of course, knew the name of *le boucher de Lyon*, all were surprised to learn that he had once worked in their home-town.

The reason is likely to be that Barbie's duties there did not give him the opportunity for the flamboyant style of leadership that was to make him such a familiar and hated figure in Lyon. There he used to walk the streets, spurning the use of a staff car and enjoying the fear of the citizens who used to step out of his path. Moreover, his time in Gex was in the planning period for the Final Solution. The time for mass round-ups of Jews had not yet arrived, so Barbie spent much of his time office-bound, compiling names and addresses for the day when the cattle-trucks would start to roll towards Auschwitz.

It was while he was involved in this painstaking clerical work that the event occurred which was to direct him to Lyon.

It was Sunday, 8 November and the church bells were ringing in Gex when British and American forces landed on the Algerian and Moroccan coasts of North Africa. These French possessions were under the control of Vichy and were, therefore, neutral. Pétain ordered his forces there to resist and there was fierce fighting between the Allies and the French as the British and Americans secured the territory that would give them a base for future operations against southern Europe. The fighting continued until Pétain's deputy, Admiral François Darlan, who by chance was in Algiers at the time, proclaimed himself 'Chief of State in French Africa' and ordered a ceasefire, thereby throwing his lot in with the Allies.

Three days after the North African landings Hitler ordered the execution of 'Operation Attila', a contingency plan drawn up long before to occupy the whole of France in the face of a threatened Allied invasion. Vichy protested loudly, but from then on all but the Mediterranean coastal strip was in German hands. Vichy might govern but Berlin ruled.

Within days of Attila Klaus Barbie had been moved from

Gex to the previously unoccupied city of Lyon. There he took charge of *AMT IV* (Department 4) of the *Sicherheitsdienst*, the SS security service.

The other SD departments were: *Amt I*: administration; *Amt II*: police liaison; *Amt III*: censorship and propaganda; *Amt V*: criminal police. Of all of them, *Amt IV* was the most powerful and worst feared, for it was the Gestapo. It, too, was subdivided: *Amt A*: anti-Communist repression; *Amt B*: repression of Freemasons and 'unacceptable' religious sects; *Amt C*: frontiers, passports; *Amt D*: anti-Jewish repression; *Amt E*: tracking down clandestine radios, codes, etc.

One of Barbie's first acts on arrival in the ancient capital of the Rhône *département* that sits astride the Rhône and Saône rivers was to organise himself some living quarters. He spent some time looking round the narrow streets of the silk town, France's fourth city and the world's gastronomic capital, before making his choice – the luxurious Hôtel Terminus beside Perrache station in the city centre. The four-star hotel, with its marble floors, gilded mirrors and exquisite wood panelling, would make a congenial HQ with ample accommodation for him and his men and plenty of spare bedrooms that could be converted into interview rooms or temporary cells. Though he maintained an office in the Terminus, he used as his private office a requisitioned house just round the corner in rue Paul Lintier.

Soon he was also working at another Gestapo HQ – a mile away across the Rhône in the grim, fortress-like École Santé Militaire. This sprawling building, where French Army doctors were once trained, suited his purposes even better than the Terminus, for its military style of architecture was more easily convertible into a prison and its warren of offices ideal for making into torture chambers.

Not far away was the military prison of Montluc with its high walls, iron gates and rows of tiny, chill cells. It was easy to guard and, like the Hôtel Terminus, close to a railhead for when the transportations to the camps began. Barbie added Montluc to his list, well satisfied with his plans.

The butcher had chosen his slaughterhouses.

By the time Barbie arrived in Lyon the French people had long since woken up to the fact that Père Pétain had betrayed them, for by now the new Reign of Terror was well under way.

It had begun back in August 1941 when two men shot and killed a German naval cadet called Moser in a Paris Métro station. The Germans had responded with an announcement that French hostages would be taken and, in the event of any future assassinations, would be executed. They also demanded that Vichy should condemn six Communists to death as a reprisal. Far from protesting at such arbitrary ruthlessness, Vichy officials assured the Germans that not only would six Communists be duly done to death but that the sentences would be carried out by guillotine in public in a central Paris square – a macabre refinement for which the Nazis had not asked.

There was no proof that Moser's killers were Communists, but the victims were chosen from their ranks because of the sudden upsurge in Communist resistance since Hitler's June 1941 attack on Russia. Until then many of France's Communists – like their comrades in Britain – had accepted Hitler as an ally of Stalin and, in some cases, had tried to sabotage the Allied war effort with strikes and subversion. Once Hitler turned on Stalin the Communists entered the Resistance fray with a will, though they tended to plough their own furrow with little reference to other underground groups. They soon became unpopular with the rest because of their taste for assassinating Germans. The resultant reprisals did not worry them overmuch because, as followers of an international cause rather than that of France, they were Communists first and Frenchmen second.

Vichy responded with even more repressive laws. Interior Minister Pierre Pucheu organised three special police units which almost mirrored those of the Gestapo – the Anti-Communist Police, the Police for Jewish Affairs and the

Police for Secret Societies. Special tribunals were convened in order that such undesirables could be sentenced with the maximum expediency and the minimum of legal niceties. This home-grown repression was designed to show the Germans that the French could be every bit as effective as the occupying power, if not more so. By these means Vichy sought to cling to some vestige of self-determination in security matters and thus show its citizens that such draconian measures were, at least, French. In the end the regime fell hopelessly between two stools — the sterner treatment neither stopped the Resistance nor changed German determination to take on the direction of public order.

Before long the Germans were shooting hostages without any reference to the French and had issued their infamous *code des ôtages* which decreed that for every German killed, between 50 and 100 Frenchmen would be executed. Within a few months more than 500 had been shot, often in public, in reprisals for Resistance activities.

Each shot, each deportation of a father, son, brother or husband for forced labour in Germany, each round-up of Jewish men, women and children, strengthened the unbridgeable gap of hatred between the French and their conquerors.

As the scales fell from her eyes France began to fight back.

Chapter 3

FRANCE

Destiny endowed Charles de Gaulle with the name by which his country had been known in ancient times. It also chose him to restore to the nation the pride and honour which had been cast aside by men whose weakness, ambition and stupidity had delivered their fellow-countrymen into a new Dark Age. In the span of four years Charles of Gaul was to become Charles of France.

Born in Lille on 22 November 1890, the son of a university professor, de Gaulle had become a professional soldier, graduating from the École Militaire de Saint-Cyr, France's Sandhurst, where his lanky 6 ft 4 in frame earned him the nickname 'Long Asparagus'. Shy, aloof and autocratic, the young lieutenant fought in the Great War with the 33rd Infantry Regiment – commanded by one Colonel Philippe Pétain – and distinguished himself as a brave and effective officer. In 1916 Captain de Gaulle was badly wounded and captured by the Germans at the Battle of Verdun. Believing him to be dead, Pétain – promoted general – wrote a citation for the posthumous award of the Legion of Honour in which he said de Gaulle was '. . . reputed for his high intellectual and moral qualities. He is an officer without equal in every respect.' It is one of history's odd quirks that those very qualities so admired by General Pétain in 1916 were the same ones that would bring about his disgrace and downfall less than three decades later.

In 1934, as Hitler tightened his grasp for power, de Gaulle published an almost prophetic military study in which he described his vision of the army of the future – one of fast-moving armoured divisions supported by a highly mobile, mechanised infantry. It struck no chords in the minds of the French General Staff who, having learned nothing from the Great War, had proclaimed the cumbersome Maginot Line as France's best means of defence in the east and then sunk back into its pre-1914 torpor. In Germany, however, then re-arming under its dynamic Führer in blatant defiance of the Treaty of Versailles, de Gaulle's study was read avidly by staff officers who saw in it much that accorded with their own views of a new kind of lightening war called *Blitzkrieg*. . . .

By May 1940, as a *général de brigade* commanding the 4th Motorised Division, de Gaulle was using these tactics to good effect when he launched successful counter-attacks against the Germans at Laon and Abbeville. On 6 June he became Under-Secretary for National Defence and War under Premier Reynaud but nine days later, when Reynaud resigned to make way for Pétain, de Gaulle walked out of office and escaped to London. From there he made an historic broadcast on the BBC in which he exhorted the French to rally to his national committee in exile. 'I tell you nothing is lost for France,' he said. 'The very same means that conquered us can be used one day to give us victory. For France is not alone. She is not alone!'

Vichy promptly sentenced him to death *in absentia* for treason and desertion. The general responded by announcing the formation in Britain of a volunteer legion – forerunner of the Free French – and broadcast appeals for his fellow-countrymen to join him in exile. It was a recruiting campaign that was to bring a steady stream of volunteers across the Channel throughout the war.

While they enlisted and donned uniforms to train alongside exiles from other conquered nations, a more clandestine recruitment was stirring in France herself as patriots banded together into a Secret Army to fight the invaders from within. At the start it was a ragbag army, a myriad collection of groups without training or equipment, who seemed to spend almost as much time quarrelling with each other as they did opposing *les Boches*. Such wranglings were inevitable in a country as politically aware as France, for each Resistance group was fired with its own vision of France's destiny after the Germans had been kicked out. Under the banners of Gaullism, socialism, Marxism, left, right, centre and every other shade of the political spectrum they rallied, each with different notions of how to oppose the Nazis.

The prickly de Gaulle, who was not without his own post-war political aspirations, grew exasperated with the in-fighting, jealousies and downright Gallic bloody-mindedness that plagued the embryonic Resistance movement. The British, uneasy hosts to the proud general, were even more exasperated — both by the internal brawling and by de Gaulle's cold arrogance. London felt the French had cut and run when the going had got too tough; that de Gaulle ought to be grateful to Britain for fighting on alone; and that, frankly, he ought to shut his mouth and do as he was told. The general had a different perspective. To him it was the British who had turned and run, leaving France to chaos, and who were now trying to dictate to him France's destiny — an entity of which he believed himself to be sole custodian. As Churchill wrote: 'He had to be rude to the British to prove to French eyes that he was not a British puppet. He certainly carried out his policy with perseverance.'

The general, acutely aware of British impatience at the inability of the French to find some unity of purpose, defined the problem in his own wry fashion: 'It is impossible in normal times to rally a nation that has 265 different kinds of cheese.' But times were far from normal and rally France he must if she were to be saved from the Nazis. His place, however, was in London, picking his way through the minefield of Anglo-French *entente* that as often as not was far from *cordiale*. He needed an emissary, someone with stature and courage, to return to France to bind the weak and tangled threads of resistance into a single rope stout enough to hang the Germans.

The man he chose was Jean Moulin.

Four centuries ago in an orchard in Provence the mystic Michel Nostradamus wrestled with obscure, allegorical and pun-riddled verses within which were hidden prophecies of such startling accuracy that, even today, many of them defy explanation. One foretold of a scourge of Europe called 'Hister': 'A leader of greater Germany will come to give false help.' And: 'There will be let loose living, deadly fire, hidden in horrible, terrifying globes.'

These warnings of the rise of Hitler and the Blitz were written close by Saint-Andiol, the small village south of Avignon where Jean Moulin, the youngest of three sons of a professor, grew up. Born on 20 June 1899, Jean's upbringing was happy and comfortable. But in early middle age he was to discover at first hand the truth of the miseries which Nostradamus had so accurately predicted in the orchard just down the road.

Though he was an accomplished artist and a deft cartoonist, Moulin chose to enter the public service. He was soon selected to join the cabinet of the prefect of Montpellier to advise on the formulation and execution of policy. Handsome and charming, he moved easily in the corridors of power. His incisive brain made him a first-rate administrator and he quickly rose in rank until, at the early age of 26, he was promoted to under-prefect at Albertville in Savoy. There he met and married a beautiful blonde girl, Marguerite Cerutti, but the marriage was a failure. Tiring of life in the provinces she departed for Paris. Two years after the wedding they were divorced.

In December 1932 Moulin entered the mainstream of international politics with a post at the Foreign Office in Paris. From 1934 to 1938 he was *chef de cabinet* to Pierre Cot, Minister for Air, a period during which, by chance, he first became involved in the world of cloak and dagger. The Spanish Civil War was raging. Franco's right-wing rebellion against the Popular Front government was being bankrolled by the Germans and Italians and Moulin discovered that a pro-Franco official in the Air Ministry was planning to do his bit for the general by smuggling a French warplane to Franco's forces. Moulin had watched the upsurge of Fascism with dismay and sympathised with the beleaguered Popular Front. He summoned the official and told him he knew of his plan, then blackmailed him into smuggling a dozen aircraft to the Republicans as the price of his silence.

In January 1939 Moulin became France's youngest prefect, taking charge of the *département* of Eure-et-Loire and working at the prefecture in the great cathedral city of Chartres, south-west of Paris. By June 1940 the ancient city was in a shambles. Tens of thousands of refugees and retreating troops passed through, fleeing westwards from the advancing Nazis and leaving in their wake a trail of dead, dying and wounded. Throughout this torrent of misery Moulin remained at his post. He saved the water supplies, rounded up doctors and nurses to care for the sick, made sure the burning buildings were doused and organised burial parties for the dead.

On 17 June the advancing Germans found near Chartres a pile of shattered corpses, mainly women and children, and demanded that the prefect sign a declaration that they had been massacred and mutilated by French West African soldiers. There was not a shred of evidence. To Moulin the bodies looked like air-raid victims and, in any case, he was not going to put his official name to such a propaganda plum for the Germans. He refused to sign. He was arrested and was tortured and beaten for several hours before being flung into a locked stone hut for the night. Fearing that more brutality might force him to sign the false document, he cut his throat with a triangle of broken glass he found on the floor. At dawn a sentry spotted his body lying in a pool of blood, the ragged neck wound still bleeding. Moulin was rushed to hospital, stitched up and given blood transfusions. Within twenty-four hours he had insisted on returning to duty. 'I can still be of some use,' he told doctors. Impressed by his protest the Germans dropped the matter of the muti-lated bodies and allowed him to resume charge of the prefecture. He was wearing — as he was to wear for the rest of his life — a scarf to hide the ugly scar on his throat.

In autumn 1940 Moulin ignored a decree from the new Vichy government to all prefects, instructing them to dismiss from office all left-wing mayors within their jurisdiction. He was immediately relieved of his post and placed on half pay. When he had cleared out his desk in the prefecture and said farewell to his staff, he was surprised to find that the Germans — who had grown to respect his competence and fairness — had mounted a guard of honour to see him off to the station. As a bonus they gave him an *Ausweiss*, a pass which enabled him to cross the border into Unoccupied France.

Jobless, he returned to the family home at Saint-Andiol and ostensibly devoted his time to painting and a little lucrative art-dealing. But in reality he was quietly gathering information about the Resistance in the south. When he had the facts he wanted, he acquired false papers in the name of Joseph Mercier and began laying his plans to join de Gaulle in London.

His false passport had an entry visa to the USA. What it lacked, however, was an exit visa from France, which had twice been refused by an official in Nice. Moulin solved the problem in typical bold fashion. He called at the man's office during a public holiday, walked past the dozing *concierge* and rummaged through the desk until he found the visa stamp. Then he rubber-stamped his false passport and tiptoed out.

For six months 'Monsieur Mercier' worked at acquiring Spanish and Portuguese transit visas and, by the time he got them, he detected four main Resistance groups. The heads of three of them — *Liberté, Libération Nationale* and *Libération* — authorised him to negotiate with de Gaulle on their behalf. The fourth group, the Communists, stayed aloof, preferring to engage in violent direct action to divert German efforts from the Russian Front. Moulin reasoned that unless the other three groups quickly received support from de Gaulle and the Allies, any would-be resisters would inevitably be driven into the arms of the Communists.

That was the warning which Moulin impressed on the general when he finally reached London, via Lisbon, in October 1941. Though the two men had never met before, they took to each other from the start, each recognising in the other similar qualities of pride, honour and devotion to France. By 4 November de Gaulle had signed a directive naming Moulin as the delegate in southern France to the Gaullist committee of national liberation – and his personal representative.

After a hasty course in parachuting at Ringway, near Manchester, Moulin took off for France on New Year's Day 1942, and in the early hours of Friday, 2 January, dropped near Arles, a few miles from Saint-Andiol. For fourteen months he travelled around France, secretly meeting the leaders of various Resistance groups. To them he was 'Max' or 'Rex'; few, if any, knew his real identity and he took painstaking precautions to ensure his anonymity. Slowly he rallied the groups to de Gaulle's cause and set up the network to distribute arms and ammunition, to gain intelligence for the Allies and to disrupt German communications with sabotage. Throughout 1942 and the first half of 1943 Moulin produced impressive results. He founded a committee to work on the judicial and constitutional problems of reconstructing the Republic; organised a group of trusted senior civil servants to design means of keeping the machinery of State running after the collapse of Vichy; and formed a general staff for the military direction of the Secret Army.

The chief of this general staff, chosen by de Gaulle, was a retired soldier, General Delestraint, who accompanied Moulin to Paris for the historic first meeting of the new national Resistance council, *Conseil National de la Résistance*. The meeting, chaired by 'Max', was held at private dining-rooms at 48 rue du Four on the evening of Thursday, 27 May 1943. It was a tribute to Moulin's determination and diplomacy that even the Communists were there, having been finally persuaded to join the CNR.

After the meeting, the first step in unifying the Resistance, Moulin headed for Lyon, leaving General Delestraint, whose cover name was 'Vidal', to set about forging a general staff. Among those he wanted to consult was the railway saboteur René Hardy, chief of 'Résistance Fer', who had developed a massive plan for the systematic disruption of France's SNCF rail network after D-Day.

The general's chief of staff, Henri Aubry, told his secretary to inform Hardy of the proposed meeting at Muette métro station at 9 a.m. on Wednesday, 9 June. The method she chose was a letter 'in clear' to a Resistance 'letter box' in rue Bouteille, Lyon. This was an astonishing decision as most Resistants (including Aubry) knew that Barbie's team had 'burned' the letter box some time earlier; in other words, they knew of its existence and kept a constant watch to intercept messages. Though Aubry knew the dangers, did his secretary? She later maintained that she did not, but never satisfactorily explained why the message to Hardy (whose cover name was 'Didot') was sent 'in clear' rather than in code. It was to be just the start of a chapter of misfortunes about which controversy rages in France to this day.

The 63-year-old general kept the appointment, striding briskly into the station entrance, wearing a beret and the rosette of the Légion d'Honneur in his buttonhole. But the man who sidled up to him, murmuring the correct cover names, was not Hardy. His name was René Saumandre, a French double-agent in the pay of the *Abwehr*, who completely took the general in with his subterfuge, so much so that the old soldier confided in him that their meeting had to be a short one as, thirty minutes later, he had a rendezvous with two more Secret Army men at the rue Pompe station.

The traitor must have found it hard to believe his luck. Not just one, but three prisoners would shortly be delivered to his masters.

As the two men drew level with a parked car, Saumandre grabbed Delestraint and bundled him into the back seat. He was driven at high speed to Gestapo HQ in avenue Foch where he was interrogated without a break for fifty gruelling hours, at the end of which he admitted to being General Delestraint, head of the Secret Army. He was subsequently transported to Germany and died in Dachau, Hitler's proto-type concentration camp on the outskirts of Munich.

The two men at the rue Pompe station were also arrested. Three valuable prisoners in one morning. The coup was a triumph for the Gestapo. For Moulin it was a sickening setback, proof, if proof were needed, that traitors had wormed their way into the fabric of the Resistance. With a heavy heart he called a meeting of southern unit command-ers to choose a successor to General Delestraint.

The venue was to be the home of Dr Frédéric Dugougon, a Resistance worker and a general practitioner, in place Castellane, Caluire, a small town high on a hill overlooking a bend of the Saône River on the northern outskirts of Lyon. The date selected was the day after Moulin's forty-fourth birthday – Monday, 21 June, 1943.

Klaus Barbie had been in Lyon for seven months and had used the time effectively to band together a small army of informers and collaborators, all bribed generously with money and property 'requisitioned' from Jews and other 'clients' of the Gestapo. Along with the greedy beating a path to Barbie's door came the political fanatics, Nazi converts and anti-Semites, all eager to denounce enemies real or imagined, or simply to settle old scores. Auguste Moritz, a Gestapo man who served with Barbie at that time, recalls queues forming daily at the kiosks installed in the centre of Lyon to receive denunciations. 'We had so many we couldn't begin to check them all out,' he said. In South America, years later, Barbie himself revealed: 'It really wasn't too hard a job being a Gestapo officer in France. The

French almost fell over themselves to give us information . . . and then their policemen carried out the arrests for us.' Several fortunes were made out of blood money during this inelegant period of Lyonnaise history and when, forty years on, Barbie was returned forcibly to the city, more than one respected senior citizen quailed at the prospect of embarrassing revelations at the Gestapo man's trial.

In addition to the ranks of paid informers the *Obersturmführer* had built round him his own personal empire. He had arrived in Lyon with a staff of about thirty including specialist technicians trained to track down illicit radio broadcasts. By 1943 he commanded between 150 and 200, about fifty of whom were Germans. The remainder were French Nazis and members of the *milice*, the French 'Gestapo'.

All of them, French and Germans alike, had orders to hunt down a man known only as 'Max'.

Barbie's power in Lyon was almost absolute, tempered only by the presence of an overall SD commander, Major Dr Knab, in the Hôtel Terminus. But Knab, being pressed by his superiors to step up the programme of Jewish deportations which had fallen woefully behind schedule, had no intention of dampening the enthusiasm of his eager young Gestapo chief. When Barbie arrived from Gex on 11 November some 42,000 Jews had been shipped from France to Auschwitz, less than half the number which Eichmann had been promised. With ill-tempered mutterings emanating from Himmler about inefficiency in France, Knab was only too pleased to let Barbie have his head.

The *Obersturmführer's* team regarded their boss – known to all as 'the Chief' – with a mixture of fear and respect, knowing too well the mercurial swings of mood that could change him from smiling affability to violent rage. To those who were seasoned policemen, he was a flamboyant amateur, a 'flash' youngster who used brute force instead of guile and who, consequently, was likely to botch a job when subtler means might have triumphed. There were murmurings among the SS NCO's that Barbie's slow promotion – he was still only a lieutenant – was due to the fact that he had failed to give any advance warning of a massive General Strike organised by the Communist Party in protest against the mass round-ups of Jews which had brought Amsterdam to a total standstill in February 1941. And all remembered uneasily the day that Barbie had summarily executed one of his own number – an SS officer who had raped a local girl. Over drinks in the Lyon bars he often recounted the story with relish. 'I told the man: "This evening at six o'clock you're to be in the cellar with the rest of the officers. There will be a rope and you are going to hang yourself." And he did it. I, myself, kicked the chair from under him.' Yet he could turn on the charm when he wanted to, smiling and joking with his staff and asking after their families as he passed them on the corridors of the Terminus or the École Santé Militaire.

With something of a reputation as a *bon viveur*, Barbie made the most of Lyon's world-famous cuisine and most evenings made a tour of the best restaurants around rue Mercière and the quays of the Saône. His favourites were the Grillon, Les Glaces, Balbo's or the Lapin Blanc. There was always a table for *le Chef* and his SS cronies or current girlfriend when, after a few drinks, he had finally chosen the restaurant whose bill of fare best suited him that evening.

After a time, tiring of living in a gloomy suite above his office in the Hôtel Terminus, he requisitioned two neighbouring houses in a smart street and set himself up in luxury with a string of mistresses and a well-stocked wine cellar. Small surprise, then, that throughout his entire service in France he only once returned on leave to Trier to see Regina and baby Ute. From his new residence he would always walk, on fine days at least, to the Terminus or stride across the Galliéni bridge over the Rhône to the École Santé Militaire, a familiar and feared figure past whom people walked with their eyes firmly fixed on the ground.

Working with Barbie most days was his interpreter, Gottlieb Fuchs, a Swiss who was nine years older than the Chief and who had been recruited by him into the German Occupation Forces administration service. This was only one of Barbie's many gaffes that give lie to the legend of the super-efficient, machine-like Gestapo officer, for Fuchs was actually a Swiss agent who, until his arrest in 1943, regularly passed information back to his country's secret service, a job which, unwittingly, Barbie made ludicrously easy for him.

In July 1983 I met Fuchs – then 79 and still suffering from the privations of Buchenwald and Belsen – at his home in Saint-Gall on the Swiss shore of Lake Constance. He recalled his first meeting with Barbie.

I was in Paris and had replied to a newspaper advert for an interpreter. It was May 1942 and I was told to report to an office in the centre of the city. There I met Barbie. He was in a dark suit and was extremely elegant, though not very tall. He asked me about myself for a few minutes and then said: 'Now, Herr Fuchs, please get ready. We are leaving for Gex in two hours.'

We climbed into a black Citroën and Barbie took the wheel with me beside him. He drove very sedately, chatting in a friendly fashion as he navigated his way out of Paris, heading south-east towards Dijon. It was a windy day with a watery red sun.

Barbie was in good spirits – really excellent humour. As we began to climb the mountain passes into the Jura he was humming a jaunty marching song. He broke off and smiled. 'Do you know it?' he asked. 'I used to sing it when I was in the Hitler Youth. Ah – those are the only memories of my younger days that count.'

Then he began to explain his philosophy. 'You know, Herr Fuchs, we will institute a New Order in Europe, a society where everyone will have work and prosperity. We have a magnificent future and those who fight alongside

Germany will take their rightful share of it. Let us hope
that the French will understand that. All good Germans
are National Socialists. Hitler is Germany and Germany
is Hitler.'

Throughout Barbie's six-month tour in Gex, Fuchs worked
on translating documents at the German *Kommandatur* in
the Château Prévessin. When Barbie was transferred to
Lyon one of his first moves was to arrange for Fuch's posting
to his staff. His own French was good, albeit strongly
accented, but the use of an interpreter gave him more
thinking time during sessions of questioning.

Fuch's arrival in Lyon was a lively affair which brought
near-panic to the Gestapo headquarters. From Gex he had
brought with him a small case containing food, for in those
uncertain days it was not wise to travel anywhere without
emergency rations. He had just been escorted to the door of
Barbie's office and was waiting to enter when he decided to
leave his case in the corridor.

Barbie rose from behind his desk with a beaming smile
and an outstretched hand. 'Ah, Herr Fuchs – how nice to see
you. . . .' he began, but was interrupted by hoarse cries of
alarm from outside the room. He stuck his head round the
door and demanded to know what the row was about. An
excitable corporal began yelling: 'Chief! Chief! We've found
something suspicious out here . . . it could be a bomb!'

Fuchs stepped past Barbie and identified the cause of
alarm as his case, which he snatched up and carried into the
room.

The Chief paled and shouted: 'Don't touch it! Are you
mad? You don't know what it is. What the. . . .' his voice
tailed into silence as the Swiss undid the catches and
brought out a cooked duck which he held out to Barbie.

'Just a little titbit I brought you from the farm at Château
Prévessin,' he said.

Barbie smiled wanly, subsided into his chair and began
gnawing at the duck. Fear had done nothing to blunt his

considerable appetite – though only 29 he already had the beginnings of a pot belly – and he had reduced the bird to a pile of bones by the time he had finished catching up on the gossip from Gex.

He lit a cigarette and slid a pass across the desk to the interpreter. It read: 'The bearer is an employee of the German Security Service. His right of passage is necessary for the Service and every facility must be given to him in all circumstances.'

Fuchs tried to hide his excitement as he read the words on the small oblong of pasteboard. Such a *carte blanche* would be a heaven-sent gift on his forthcoming missions for the Swiss Secret Service.

Even better was to come.

'Your job, among others, is to provide supplies of meat and vegetables for our mess here in the hotel,' Barbie explained. 'I want you to get the stuff in the region around Gex. The produce there is good and, as you know, you can reach Gex from here by cutting through Switzerland. While you're there I want you to buy all the newspapers you can and, in Geneva, keep your ear to the ground for any news you think might interest me.'

Armed with a thick wad of banknotes doled out by Barbie from the ever-full petty cash tin, Fuchs set off with a car and driver for Gex, crossing the border on the outskirts of Geneva and dropping down into the city centre. There he bought as many newspapers and periodicals as he could lay his hands on before crossing back into France at the border post at Ferney-Voltaire to sort out some black-market contacts in Gex. The meat, fruit and vegetables they sold him were top quality, better than anything to be found in the shops of Lyon, but horrendously expensive – ten times the price fixed by the Vichy government.

When he returned to the Hôtel Terminus he apologised for overspending. Barbie nodded approvingly at his wares and patted him on the shoulder. 'Don't worry, Herr Fuchs,' he said. 'This is good stuff, just what we need. And forget about the cost—there's plenty more money where that came from.'

'By the way, I'd be grateful if you could do me a favour on your next trip. I'd like to send some little gifts to my wife and daughter – some cheese, sweets and perhaps some Swiss chocolate. Do you think you could bring some back with you?'

A few days later Fuchs returned with a pile of foreign newspapers and periodicals, plus a Swiss cheese, some bars of chocolate and half a kilo of boiled sweets. Barbie was delighted.

'What address in Trier shall I send it to, Chief?' asked Fuchs.

'Liebfrauenstrasse . . .' Barbie began. Then: 'Oh – no, hang on. Don't send them from here. An SS officer on a special mission should not be sending packets of sweets to his family. I've a friend who's a customs officer; I'll get him to deliver them.'

A week or so later Barbie showed Fuchs a letter from his wife in which she discreetly acknowledged receipt of the parcel with the line, 'We have been visited by a family friend,' Proudly the Gestapo man handed over a picture of 18 month-old Ute tucking into her first piece of Swiss chocolate.

Despite this sentimental demonstration of husbandly and fatherly affection, Barbie was far from being the devoted family man. Within weeks of arriving in Lyon he had acquired a formidable reputation as a rake. He was young and good-looking, and the power he wielded was a strong aphrodisiac to many women, Germans and French alike, who used to squabble among themselves for the privilege of sitting on the Chief's knee when he was interrogating suspects. In the early days there were few signs of the brutalities which were to become his hallmark. Though he carried with him a riding crop, he seemed to use it for nothing more sinister than tickling the legs of his bevy of admirers. When, before long, Barbie began resorting to cruel torture to extract confessions there were even more volunteers willing to sit in his lap and enjoy his caresses, strange young women to whom the screams and blood gave an extra sexual charge.

One of his first conquests in Lyon was a Gestapo secretary-interpreter, Thedy Scheffer, a good-looking and statuesque blonde of around 40, who was quickly introduced to Barbie's bed and who became besotted with him. Fuchs was her confidante and on many mornings she would regale him with lurid and detailed accounts of the previous night's love-making. She was forever hanging round in the corridor, asking, 'How's the Chief?' or 'What's he doing now, Herr Fuchs?'

The unfortunate Thedy had a sexual appetite which needed constant nourishment and, though she realised quickly that she was merely Barbie's standby when he couldn't be bothered to seek younger conquests, she was almost pathetically grateful for his attentions. One night, when he was out on the town womanising, she suggested to Fuchs that he might like to take her to bed. The interpreter, well aware of his boss's hair-trigger temper, wisely pleaded a headache.

'He never really had a favourite,' Fuchs recalled. 'Thedy was always there and often ended up in his bed, but there was also "Mimiche", a ravishing blonde whose real name was Antoinette Morlot, and a dark-haired one who was supposed to be the mistress of Marcel Moyne, head of the Gestapo's French section. Barbie took her to bed quite often. One night it was one woman, the next another. He wasn't choosy and used to go on the prowl like an alleycat for anything that was available.

'One morning in the office I saw him and an *Unterscharführer* [sergeant] sniggering over a pile of photographs, all of nude women taken at an orgy in Grenoble a few nights earlier. One was of a very good-looking woman spreadeagled on a bed. I said I thought she was a nice-looking piece of stuff.

' "Too right, Herr Fuchs," said the sergeant. "And do you

know who she is? She's the wife of a French colonel. She was the Chief's bit at the party and he says she gave him a hell of a good time." '

Though Lyon was only one of twenty-two regional command headquarters of the German security service in France, the city's reputation as the 'Resistance capital' gave Barbie's operation a unique importance. His operatives were frequently detached for temporary duties elsewhere in the country. One such occasion was an order from Gestapo HQ in avenue Foch asking for two of Barbie's agents to operate in the capital in an attempt to flush out a British agent known to be working there. Barbie selected the loyal Thedy – perhaps to get her out of Lyon while he bedded his latest conquest – and one of his deputies, *Untersturmführer* Schmelzer. He briefed them carefully. They were to take the train to Paris and, posing as man and wife, check into a certain hotel, believed by the Gestapo to be a contact point for the Briton.

Well-heeled with money from the petty cashbox, the two boarded the express at Perrache station and promptly made for the buffet car where they ordered wine. By the time they were nearing Paris's southern outskirts they were wildly, hopelessly drunk, howling with mirth and yelling for yet more drink. When the train pulled into the Gare de Lyon they could barely stand. Clinging to each other for support and laughing uproariously, they lurched unsteadily along the platform, cannoning into other passengers and bouncing off luggage trolleys. They fell into a taxi which delivered them to the hotel. There, arms wrapped around each other, they weaved into the foyer, signed the register and demanded champagne. Champagne was brought. Long into the night the party pursued its noisy course as neighbouring guests tried vainly to sleep through the shouts of glee and snatches of song. Finally the ever-willing Thedy dragged Schmelzer on to the bed for a prolonged and uninhibited bout of love-making.

They woke next morning with titanic hangovers only to

discover that, in the aftermath of their alcoholic passion, someone had sneaked into their room and had stolen all their money, their false papers and even their clothes. The Paris police were called, there was a solemn period of note-taking and the two were driven to police headquarters. There Schmelzer dropped his cover story and tried to convince the bunch of sceptical *gendarmes* that he was a Gestapo officer. Finally he persuaded them to telephone Barbie in Lyon.

Barbie, dragged from his bed to vouch for his two agents, became speechless with fury, well aware that the uproar in the hotel would have scared off every British agent for miles around. An officer was dispatched to Paris to bring back 'those drunken bastards', and that night they stood pale and woebegone before the Chief's desk, flinching before the almost incoherent torrent of abuse. Rigidly at attention, Schmelzer took the verbal flaying and almost broke down when Barbie handed out his punishment – a posting to the Russian Front. Thedy wept and howled as Barbie screamed that she was a 'drunken nymphomaniac' whose only sense lay between her legs and threatened to have her sent to a soldiers' brothel.

His temper vented, he stumped off in search of a drink, vowing that next time there was an important job in Paris he would do it himself.

But for the fluttering swastika flags and the throng of German uniforms in the streets, it could have been the old pre-war Paris that sparkled so gaily in the bright sunshine of a crisp winter's morning in January 1943. Josephine Butler, a 42-year-old English doctor, educated in France and trained at the Sorbonne, sipped her coffee at a pavement café in the Champs-Élysées and scanned the crowds for a glimpse of the face which she was seeking. Butler was a British agent, codenamed 'Jay Bee' and the only woman member of Churchill's elite 'Secret Circle', a tiny and select band of handpicked operatives, the existence of which was not known even to the War Office or MI5. Each had been chosen by Churchill himself and reported directly to him, for the Prime Minister had long feared that the usual agencies of the Secret Intelligence Service had been infiltrated by double-agents. The Circle was his own inner guard of agents, assigned to his own pet intelligence missions. If no one else knew of their existence, he reasoned, no one could betray them.

Dr Butler had recently flown over by night from England in a Lysander. Her brief was to discover the whereabouts of Admiral Wilhelm Canaris, head of the *Abwehr*, the German military intelligence agency, who was then visiting Paris. Canaris, a monarchist and officer of the 'old school', was known to disapprove of Hitler and his henchmen and might, the British believed, be persuaded to help overthrow the Nazis, thus easing the way to a possible end of the war.* Butler's brief was not to contact Canaris, simply to monitor his movements and relay them to London.

At a nearby table three uniformed Gestapo officers sat talking and smoking over coffee and cognac.

'Presently an old man came along, head down, searching in the gutter,' Dr Butler, then 82, recalled in 1983.

He was obviously hunting for cigarette ends — cigarettes were virtually unobtainable at that time. As he reached the front of the café one of the officers threw down a half-finished cigarette. The old man pounced on it, but before he could straighten up another Gestapo officer stepped forward, pressed his foot on to the back of the wretched man's neck and went on pressing until his victim blacked out.

I could imagine the cruel power of that jack-booted

---

*Canaris did, indeed, plot to overthrow Hitler and was subsequently executed for treason. The information which led to his arrest came from Russia who, though at war with Germany, did not want any separate peace between London and Berlin. Moscow received the tip-off from a Russian agent in the British Secret Service — one Harold 'Kim' Philby.

foot. It was not removed until it had casually crushed out a life. Smiling, the officer turned away and called an elderly waiter to get rid of the body.

Numbed and sickened by what she had seen, Dr Butler sat, unable to move. A minute later, unaware of what had just happened, an old cripple hobbled down the pavement. He, too, was peering into the gutter. Sensing fresh fun one of the Gestapo men tossed a cigarette in the man's direction. His aim was bad and it rolled on the pavement near Dr Butler's feet. Unable to hide her disgust any longer, she stamped on it and ground it to pieces beneath her heel.

She cursed her stupidity. She had broken the first law that is drummed into every secret agent – never make yourself conspicuous.

Behind her a chair scraped. Slowly she turned to find the Gestapo officer studying her with pale, emotionless eyes. In almost perfect French he said: 'Madame, you do not like Germans.' Minutes later she was under arrest and was pushed into an office in the avenue Kléber where a dozen Gestapo men stood talking. Silence fell as she was prodded forward towards a desk at the far end of the room. Behind it, dressed in a black uniform with oak leaves on the lapel, sat a young man, obviously in charge, who listened impassively as the officers from the cafe told their story of Butler's 'insulting behaviour'. Though she did not know it at the time, it was Klaus Barbie – in Paris on a brief assignment following his subordinates' drunken fiasco.

'He was not very tall, but good-looking – rather handsome, in fact,' Dr Butler recalled. 'He had very pale blue or grey eyes that watched me intently, but he positioned himself with a window behind him so that his face was in shadow, making it difficult for me to read his expression.'

'Why do you dislike Germans?' The question was asked in French, accented and quiet.

'I did not say I disliked Germans, and I'm sorry I acted the way I did on the spur of the moment. You see, I am a schoolteacher [her cover story] and am very fond of children. I have always felt that elderly people are rather like children at times and need protecting.'

Barbie was unconvinced. 'I am inclined to believe that you are more of an aristocrat than a teacher. You are certainly very cool and collected. Where do you teach?'

She began reciting her cover story, explaining that she was a relief teacher between posts. Barbie nodded, apparently believing her, and her spirits began to rise. But then the quiet voice spoke: 'Strip!'

Dr Butler began to tremble. 'Do you mean remove all my clothes?'

'Yes – hurry up,' he snapped. 'Or would you like some help?'

There were guffaws from the other Gestapo men. Shaking with humiliation, 'Jay Bee' began to undress – hat, gloves, coat, blouse. . . . A deeply religious woman, she fumbled for the fastening of her skirt and stared into Barbie's eyes, praying to God that she would find some mercy there. She was about to lower her skirt when Barbie, with sudden impatience, barked: 'This is a waste of time. You may dress.' Quickly she did so and was about to pick up her gloves and hat when Barbie stopped her. 'Leave those! I am inclined to believe you, but you are not going yet.'

He sentenced her to two days' detention which she spent scrubbing floors, cleaning latrines and polishing the officers' jack-boots. Though she pretended not to speak German, she was fluent in the language and during her two-day stay with the Gestapo she overheard conversations about the Chief. He was, she gathered, soon to return to Lyon and some of the NCOs were hoping he would take them with him – disturbing news because Lyon was one of 'Jay Bee's' operational areas.

At the end of her sentence Barbie called her into the office and told her she had worked well. 'He hoped I realised how kind they had been to me and that I would tell my friends that the Germans wanted to help the French people and give them the advantages of the New Order.'

Anxious to get away, Dr Butler nodded as if in agreement.

'Again I noticed his very pale eyes and the quiet voice. Despite his good looks I remember thinking: "I don't think much of you, my friend." Yet in a way I was grateful. God had answered my prayers and the man had shown me mercy.'

It was a quality that was never again to manifest itself in the heart of *Obersturmführer* Nikolaus Barbie.

Chapter 4

JEAN MOULIN

It was the day of the summer solstice and a high sun cast lean shadows on the streets of the village of Caluire, a northern suburb of Lyon that clings to high ground between the Rhône and Saône rivers. Monday, 21 June 1943. The time, a little after 2.30 p.m., that unhurried post-lunch limbo when small-town France retreats behind its front doors and shuttered windows to doze off *le déjeuner* with a glass of cognac or calvados.

The streets were quiet, almost empty. Strolling without haste, the three companions chatted quietly, pausing occasionally to look in shop windows and to check that they were not being followed. One of the trio was a shortish man, good-looking and dressed in a dark suit. Despite the heat of the day, he wore a scarf knotted around his throat. . . .

A number 33 tram clanked by, grinding up the steep hill. As the sound faded the three men crossed the road in its wake and turned into a small, tree-lined square that overlooked wooded meadows sloping down to the Saône. But for a parked bicycle and a handful of squabbling sparrows, it too was empty.

Reassured, Moulin led the way through the iron gate set into the high ivy-clad wall on the eastern side of the square, ascended a short flight of steps and knocked on the door of the three-storey villa.

The time was 2.45. Jean Moulin's longest day was about to begin. . . .

The others were already there. Dr Dugougon, who owned the villa; Bruno Larat, parachute operations; Henri Aubry, chief of staff; André Lassagne, information; Colonel Albert Lacaze, whose role is unclear; and an unexpected visitor, René Hardy, who had not been invited to attend, but whom Aubry – without consulting the others – had brought along.

Dugougon was in his surgery, dealing with bona fide patients; the other five were kicking their heels in a sitting-room on the first floor, anxiously checking their watches, for the meeting had been arranged for 2 p.m. Forty-five minutes elapsed before they heard the remaining three conspirators being ushered into the hall by the maid who, mistaking them for patients, showed them into the surgery waiting-room.

None of the Resistance men there that day knew Moulin, not even the two companions who had arrived with him, Raymond Aubrac (chief of staff, southern zone) and Lieutenant-Colonel Schwarzfeld (a nominee for General Delestraint's successor as head of the Secret Army). They knew de Gaulle's emissary only as 'Max', 'Rex' or 'Regis'. That day, in fact, Moulin was using a different cover name – Jean Martel.

Close on their heels came Klaus Barbie.

Within minutes of Moulin's arrival, a posse of black Citroëns roared into place Castellane, and the door – the only one to the villa – was kicked in by heavy police boots. Upstairs, René Hardy pulled a gun from his pocket but the others yelled at him to put it away; he stood no hope of winning a shoot-out against so many Gestapo men.

Then the Germans were on them, kicking and punching, knocking heads against walls, and shouting for the prisoners to raise their hands. One by one they were handcuffed – all except Hardy who was lightly secured with a chain around his wrist, the other end of which was held by a leather-jacketed Gestapo agent. Downstairs, Moulin, Aubrac, Schwarzfeld, and a handful of terrified patients were also being rounded up. Dugougon came running out of his surgery and was stopped by a savage kick in the stomach. As he doubled up, Moulin bent over him and whispered: 'My name is Jean Martel.'

In his pocket he had a sick note made out in that name and signed by another doctor, with a letter to Dr Dugougon saying that 'M. Martel' was suffering from rheumatism and asking that he be recommended to a specialist. He tried to show it to his captors but they waved it away and all the occupants of the house, Secret Army men and the genuinely sick, were pushed into the hallway. In the mêlée Aubrac passed Moulin some of the notes he had prepared for the meeting. Chewing furiously, they managed to swallow the incriminating evidence.

That they had been betrayed there was no doubt . . . and betrayed by someone of high rank in the Secret Army, for the time and place of the meeting were facts known only to a chosen few. But who was the traitor? Today there are many people who believe that the events that occured in the seconds that followed identified him beyond a shadow of doubt.

As they were being manhandled towards the cars René Hardy, still only lightly fettered, flailed his fist into his guard's abdomen. The man folded, dropping his Mauser pistol; Hardy shouldered him aside and sprinted across the square, jinking and weaving like a snipe, towards the low wall beyond which the grassy slope led down to the river.

As he hurdled the wall, the Germans recovered their wits and opened fire with their weapons – British Stens – at the figure zig-zagging through the field. Reaching a ditch, the Frenchman dropped on to his belly and began shooting back before taking to his heels once more. One bullet found its mark, ploughing along his left arm and breaking the bone before he stumbled into the comparative safety of a clump of trees.

Though his wound hurt abominably, the 32-year-old railway saboteur kept running, dodging in and out of the trees as more bullets – all fired in single shots, rather than automatic bursts – cracked past. Beyond the copse he could see the wide, silvery ribbon of the Saône. Nearby, he knew, was a safe house where he could hide and have his wound dressed.

Hardy was a keen rugby player. Now he ran as he had never run before, on or off the rugby field. Today, forty years later, a broken and bitter wreck of a man, he is still running. . . .

Gottlieb Fuchs, Swiss double-agent and interpreter to the Gestapo in Lyon, sat at his desk in the entrance hall of the École Santé Militaire, flicking idly through a newspaper and reflecting on his changing fortunes. First, there was his new duty, dealing with members of the public at the recently requisitioned medical school's reception desk. It suited him better than the noise and bustle of the Hôtel Terminus with its incessant clattering of jack-boots, slamming of doors and the endless whistling of SS troopers in the corridors . . . always the same damned tune too: 'The Chocolate Soldier'.

Then there were his regular trips to Switzerland, a welcome break from office routine and a chance to savour some fresh air and glorious scenery, to say nothing of a God-given opportunity to slip titbits of information about the state of France under the Nazis to his friends in Swiss Intelligence. Of that arrangement Barbie, of course, knew nothing. But he was delighted with Fuch's food-foraging on the black market at Gex, his information and newspaper-gathering sorties into Geneva, and the regular supply of sweets and chocolate for Regina and Ute back home in Trier.

So delighted was he, in fact, that he had recently agreed to Fuch's request that he be allowed to rent a civilian apartment in Lyon, away from the noise that had disturbed his sleep in his gloomy bedroom in the Terminus. Not only had he granted him that privilege, he had also almost doubled the interpreter's salary to 15,000 francs a month. This newfound freedom, Fuchs maintains, enabled him to move around Lyon, mixing with its citizens and warning trusted Resistance friends of impending round-ups and Gestapo raids. It is, however, open to debate how much the Lyonnaise took on trust a man who worked so closely with *le*

Boucher and who was, in his own words, treated by him like
'a favourite dog'.

Fuchs had just turned to the sports page when he heard a
commotion, shouts and the revving of car engines, from the
big quadrangle that lay inside the wrought-iron gates of the
medical school. He slid his newspaper into his desk drawer
as he watched a grim-faced Barbie lead eight handcuffed
men, surrounded by armed guards, in through the door.
They were taken down to the cellars but soon afterwards
were moved to the military prison at Fort Montluc.

> There I was thrown into a cube-like cell, three metres by
> three [Raymond Aubrac recalls]. There was a high barred
> window and a bucket for sanitation, but nothing else – no
> chair, no bed, no blankets . . . nothing.
>   In the morning, a guard brought me some sort of hot
> liquid with a mouldy scum floating on the surface and a
> quart of water. For the rest of that day I was ignored.
>   The following day – Wednesday, 23 June – I was look-
> ing out through the grille in my cell door and, for the first
> time, saw the terrible results of Barbie's handiwork.

The man he knew as 'Max', alias 'Jean Martel', was being
dragged along the corridor by two German soldiers, unable
to stand without their support. His head, caked in blood and
roughly bandaged with a dirty cloth, lolled vacantly. His
clothes were bloodstained and hung in tatters as though
their owner had been savaged by a frenzied animal.

Next day it was Aubrac's turn. They came for him early
in the morning and drove him to the medical school where
he was 'kicked like a dog' into a cellar. Some hours later two
soldiers dragged him out and escorted him upstairs to
Barbie's office.

> They flung me into the room and slammed the door be-
> hind me. I was very frightened because I knew of the
> reputation of the Butcher of Lyon. Now here he was, sit-

ting at his desk with his back to the window.

He stood up and walked towards me. He was not very tall and a little plump, casually dressed in a summer shirt. I was 29; he was 30. He looked at me cynically, enjoying his power and my fear. I could see that his eyes were pale, but I never saw them properly because he always seemed to position himself in front of a window so that the light was behind him.

He had a length of wood in his hand which he swung casually as he began the interrogation. His questions were simple and always the same – 'Where is Bernard?' [The code name of Emmanuel d'Astier, the head of *Libération*.] 'Where are the weapons?' and 'Where is the money?'

When I did not answer he screamed 'Dirty pig!' and smashed me over the head with his piece of wood.

The blow was struck with full force. Aubrac fainted and slid to the floor. Some time later he came round to find Barbie standing over him, still shouting abuse and kicking violently at his head and stomach. A toecap caught him on the temple and merciful blackness returned.

Two or three times, as Aubrac drifted in and out of unconsciousness, he was astonished to see Barbie back in his chair with a 'very pretty woman wearing heavy make-up' sitting on his knee.

I think she was a prostitute [Aubrac recalls]. It seemed to me that Barbie had her with him to witness my beating as a way of proving his virility. I certainly got the impression that he wasn't particularly interested in getting answers from me, but simply enjoyed the sadism and the torture.

He was not a good policeman, you see. Brutal and cruel – yes, but a good copper – no.

First he never found my true identity or even realised that I was Jewish, yet all he had to do was to have me undress to see that I was circumcised.

Second, he allowed my wife to fool him so much that she was able to arrange my escape.

Third, and his worst error, he tortured to death Jean Moulin, a man of very great importance, a leading politician. Though I am certain that Moulin would never have talked, he could have been used in other ways, as a hostage for example.

Barbie wasn't a policeman; he was primeval.

For three dreadful, pain-clouded months Aubrac stood up to the regular beatings and threats. For a time at Montluc he shared a cell with a boy of 16 or 17 who had been in a coma since his skull had been fractured during interrogation. The youngster died in his arms, mumbling the name of Barbie over and over again. When, by September, Aubrac had still confessed nothing, the Gestapo chief lost patience and sentenced him to death.

Next day Gottlieb Fuchs looked up from his desk at the medical school to find a haughty and obviously pregnant young woman standing over him, demanding in a loud voice to see *Obersturmführer* Barbie. Her name, she said, was Ghislaine de Barbentane. The Germans are a rank-conscious race and Barbie, imbued with all the hierarchical rigidity of the SS, was no exception. He let himself be impressed by the fact that an aristocratic lady had come to see him. Politely he ushered her into his office, offered her a chair and listened with growing astonishment as she explained the purpose of her visit.

'*Obersturmführer* Barbie,' she began, 'my father is a general and greatly admires the honour of the German Army. In our family we, too, have honour which decrees that any child which is born to the family must bear the name of his father.

'You have here a man who has been sentenced to death. This man has seduced me and, as you can see, I am carrying his child. The law of France permits a woman to marry a condemned man and I wish to marry this man.

'For this, I need your authorisation, which is why I have come to see you today. With your permission I can be married to this man, Ermeline, [Aubrac's code name] and the child will have a name.'

Barbie, flabbergasted, poured himself a glass of rum and lighted a cigarette. Then he laughed and slapped his thigh. 'By heaven, *vicomtesse*, I'll do it. You shall marry your seducer!'

Aubrac was brought from Montluc under heavy guard to hear this proposal to which, somewhat numbly, he agreed. It was arranged that the countess would return three weeks later when once again her lover would be driven from Montluc to sign the marriage contract. On the appointed day, as the prison van carrying the husband-to-be neared avenue Berthelot, there was an ambush. Soldiers of the Secret Army shot dead the driver and the two guards and spirited Aubrac away.

The attack was led by the totally bogus countess – but genuinely pregnant Lucie – Raymond Aubrac's wife since 1939. As they made their escape a witness heard Aubrac call to her: 'This is what marriage is all about, darling!'

In a towering rage, as much at being duped by a woman as by the loss of an important prisoner, Barbie swore vengeance on the 'countess' and imposed a three-day curfew on the city.

For Jean Moulin though, there was to be no escape other than that ultimate one which must come to us all one day. And for him it must have come as a benediction.

With fist and cosh, alternate scalding and freezing baths, kicks, threats and degradation, Klaus Barbie slowly and methodically broke Moulin's body, but never once his spirit. The former prefect, who had known torture once before and had sought suicide, knew that this time he would be given no chance to kill himself. He knew too that if he broke the Secret Army would be destroyed and Resistance in France would come to a virtual end. For he, unlike the others, knew the whole broad canvas. If they talked then arrests would certainly be made but the Resistance, though damaged, would continue; if he talked the whole movement would be annihilated.

It is my belief, based on what fragmented pieces of information remain after the span of forty years, that Moulin quite deliberately resolved to goad the Germans into killing him before he reached the inevitable breaking-point. A man as shrewd as he would need only a few minutes in Barbie's company to realise that the SS officer was no cold-blooded interrogator, but an unbalanced sadist who would fly into ungovernable rages when crossed. Moulin tucked away that knowledge for future use.

The day after the Caluire raid Barbie had interrogated first Dr Dugougon and then André Lassagne, whom he suspected of being 'Max'. Neither had said anything. But the next day – Wednesday – one of the prisoners let something slip under torture. As a result cell no. 130 at Montluc was immediately placed under a two-man twenty-four-hour a day guard.

Its inmate, Jean Moulin, soon realised that the Germans had singled him out as the most important member of the group. Now it was a question of preventing them from discovering just how important he really was.

All that week he was savaged, both in his cell and at the medical school, until his body was torn and bleeding. So intensive was the onslaught that it even began to tell on his tormentor, for Barbie was grey-faced and weary from the physical exertion of his torturing. Furthermore he was under severe pressure from Paris to extract from his rich haul of prisoners details of the Resistance plan for an armed insurrection when the Allied invasion began.

Towards the end of that week – probably on Thursday 24 June – Moulin made his only confession to Barbie. Barely able to speak through swollen lips and broken teeth he croaked: 'I am Max. My real name is Jean Moulin. I will say nothing else.' Barbie tried to press home his advantage with a series of questions. Moulin shook his head and maintained his stubborn silence, even when a fresh flurry of kicks and truncheon-blows battered him to the floor.

When he came round he couldn't even croak but made signs that the Gestapo men should bring him pencil and paper. Eagerly Barbie helped him into a chair and fetched some paper. On the top line he wrote in his distinctive Gothic script the name 'Jean Moulins'. Moulin took the pencil from him, unsteadily crossed out the final 's' and motioned Barbie away, hunching wearily over the sheet of paper.

Barbie gave him five minutes before he returned. Moulin held out the paper, smudged in one corner with a bloody thumbprint. Barbie took it and looked in disbelief as he saw, not the facts he sought, but a cruelly lifelike caricature of himself.

The beating began again. . . .

At around 4 p.m. on Friday 25 June, Gottlieb Fuchs, sitting alone in the reception hall of the École Santé Militaire, looked up as he heard noises at the top of the stairs leading to the first floor. He witnessed a terrible sight.

The prisoner he knew as Jacques Martel was lying on his back, spattered with blood, his feet tied together with a rope. Looped around the rope was a buckled leather belt which was held by Klaus Barbie. The Chief was jacketless and dishevelled, his fair hair was untidy and he was breathing heavily. His eyes were wild and his lips were moving as if he was talking to himself. As a man will tug at a heavy sled, he was dragging his victim behind him, descending the stairs ahead of the body whose rolling blood-soaked head bumped down each stone step with a force that made Fuchs wince.

Oblivious to the horrified stare of his interpreter, Barbie paused for breath at the bottom of the stairway before jerking at the belt to get the body moving again across the polished marble floor. Like a carcass in an abattoir, arms trailing behind its head, it moved slowly towards the stairs that led down to the cellar, leaving smears of blood in its wake.

Though Fuchs could not see the descent into the bowels of the building he once again heard the sickening and rhythmic thump-thump as the back of Moulin's skull slid down every step.

A few minutes later Barbie reappeared. His face shone with sweat. He was muttering to himself: 'That's it. That's it. If he doesn't talk tonight I'm finished with him and he can go to Paris tomorrow.' Still mumbling, he crossed the hall unsteadily and slowly plodded up the stairs towards his office.

Fuchs stepped over to the front door and called for the guard, who had slipped outside for a breath of fresh air a few minutes before the appalling scene had taken place. Though he was an SS man, Fuchs liked him and they had become quite friendly.

'I'd like to take a look in the cellar,' said the Swiss. 'I thought I heard something down there. Come with me and we'll take a look.'

They found Moulin lying on his back in a corner, his torn and bloodstained shirt lying in a heap beside him. His torso was a mass of bruises and bleeding lacerations. He was breathing raggedly through torn lips.

> I turned him on his side to stop him choking and bundled his shirt under his head as a pillow [says Fuchs]. His eyes were puffed up and closed, his face and head covered with blood. He looked ghastly. I used my handkerchief to clean his face as best I could and, as I wiped the blood away, the SS man came forward. He was obviously shaken. He reached out sympathetically and gently touched the battered face. I heard him whisper: 'One day all this wrong must come to an end.'

Next day, desperately ill with a fractured skull and brain damage, Moulin was sent to Paris. For several days he was

kept at the villa of Gestapo chief, *Sturmbannführer* Bömelburg in the suburb of Neuilly where, despite medical attention, he remained in a coma. André Lassagne and General
Delestraint were being detained at the same house. Major
Bömelburg took them to Moulin's bedside and asked: 'Don't
you recognise your friend Max?'

Lassagne shook his head. Delestraint retorted angrily:
'Military honour forbids me to recognise anyone as that poor
wreck.'

A few days later Moulin was put on a train for Germany.
Somewhere, probably near Metz, he died, on or around 9
July. No one knows for certain. Nor can anyone even be sure
that the ashes that lay in Père-Lachaise cemetery from the
end of the war until 1964 were his. In December of that year
General de Gaulle and thousands of fellow-Frenchman paid
homage to the gallant man who had unified the Resistance
as, with drawn sabres and flickering torches, the Republican
Guard escorted the ashes to the Panthéon, the last resting
place of all France's great heroes.

As Moulin's remains were placed alongside those of Vol-
taire, Rousseau and Victor Hugo, André Malraux, one of
France's leading academics, spoke this tribute: '*He made
none of the regiments: but he made the Army.*'

Barbie's coup at Caluire gave him eight trump cards, among
them the ace of spades. The fact was, though, that such a
splendid hand did not win him a single trick. And he threw
away the ace completely.

There is no doubt that at least one of the arrested men
was tortured into an admission, but gave little away except
that 'Jean Martel' was 'Max', thereby merely substituting
one code name for another. And although the German
security service knew of 'Max' as an important Resistance
figure, they did not know he was Moulin, the personal emissary of General de Gaulle.

Barbie, however, *had* discovered his true identity, but in
so doing had so smashed his body and brain that he had left

him a vegetable. His inevitable death had robbed the Gestapo of its chance of uncovering the Secret Army's battleplan. Other methods, drugs, for example, might have forced Moulin to speak, as might more subtle, less damaging methods of tortures, for it is said that every man, however, courageous, has his breaking-point.

Barbie's superiors in Paris were angry with him for having ruined a promising interrogation by his brutality. Fuchs maintains that until the end of the war Barbie kept 'Max's' real identity secret, fearing even more wrath if it was discovered that he had killed Jean Moulin. If this was true it was a bitter irony, for by his own hand he had destroyed the one capture that would have brought him fame and promotion.

Thereafter he always kept in the top drawer of his knee-hole desk a single sheet of paper which, from time to time, as Gottlieb Fuchs has commented, he would pull out and examine, as a man will look at a charm or talisman. More than once in post-war interviews Barbie referred to the drawing.

The pencilled caricature was shaky but unmistakeable. As was the bloody thumbprint in one corner. . . .

It is an August day in 1983 and the village of Melle, south-west of Poitiers, is sleeping under a blazing sun. From the fields comes the incessant murmuring of insects and the far-off puttering of a tractor.

Close by the parish church is rue de Crèvecour, a narrow alleyway of cheek-by-jowl cottages whose paintwork has been scabbed and bleached by time. Weeds sprout from between the cobbles. Number 5 is guarded by a high, ramshackle gate, beyond which a gritty path leads to the kitchen door which is ajar. The interior is gloomy, but cool after the August sun.

An old man rises with painful slowness, wheezing with bronchitis. He is still tall but, at the age of 72, stooped. The pale eyes are tired in the creased face. The hand that shakes mine is knobbled with arthritis, but steady enough as it pours two glasses of Chival Regal and passes one to me. '*Santé*'

At our feet an 11-year-old girl plays, his daughter Sophie by the smiling middle-aged woman with whom he lives. The woman sits beside him listening to his words, occasionally touching his arm to warn him that he is rambling, moving out of his reach the yellow cigarettes that are killing him and helping him to his feet on his frequent visits to the lavatory.

And each time he returns, shuffling slowly back to the table, she hears again the story she has heard countless times of a June day forty years ago when she was a child and he was a handsome young soldier; four decades of bitterness through which René Hardy has moved with the spectre of Jean Moulin hovering beside him.

Hardy's headlong flight through the woods brought him to the safe house he sought, close to the banks of the Saône. It was owned by Mme Damasse, a Resistance sympathiser, who admitted him without question and strapped up his arm so that he could hurry back to the city to warn others of the arrests at Caluire.

However, two cyclists to whom he had appealed for help reported him to the French police who arrested him and took him to the Grange-Blanche hospital for treatment, before handing him over to the Germans. They transferred him to an internment centre at Anther medical care and eventual interrogation. He escaped from there, he claims, by jumping from a second-floor window.

The Resistance men arrested at Caluire were convinced they had been betrayed by Hardy. He had been the only prisoner not handcuffed; with all the firepower available to them, the Germans had loosed off only single, aimed shots in his direction when they could have sent a withering hail of automatic fire. The conclusion was obvious: Barbie had 'turned' Hardy and then allowed him to escape as a reward for his treachery.

Lucie, Raymond Aubrac's wife, was ordered to execute him as a traitor. The method she chose was a small pot of jam liberally seasoned with cyanide which she sent in a parcel to him. Cannily Hardy anticipated such an attempt and had asked his jailers to test all the food that came to him from outside sources.

When, with apparent ease, he escaped from the internment centre, his former comrades were even more convinced that the head of 'Résistance Fer' was Barbie's creature. In 1947, Hardy was arrested and arraigned before a special court convened to deal with allegations of collaboration. After a stormy trial, which divided France, he was acquitted of Moulin's betrayal.

Soon afterwards vital new evidence came to light which Hardy had not seen fit to mention in his trial. It created a sensation which resulted in the former Resistance man appearing once again in the dock, following a statement from an ex-sleeping-car attendant on the main line Lyon–Paris route.

Through the almost criminal negligence of Henri Aubry the clear-language invitation for Hardy to meet General Delestraint at Muette métro station had been sent to the 'burned' letter box in Lyon. Hardy has always claimed that he never saw the letter because in order to have seen it he would have had to visit a letter box which he knew was being monitored by the Gestapo. Yet, by an extraordinary coincidence, he chose to visit Paris on the very same day of the métro station meeting – 9 June.

The events that followed could have come straight out of a Hollywood script. Hardy had a wagon-lit reservation for the night of 7–8 June. When he entered his compartment he found he was sharing it with a M. Cressol, a Vichy official. In the very next compartment were two of Barbie's men, former Resistance men, turned traitors – Jean Multon and Robert Moog. Their journey was on Barbie's orders . . . after reading the fatal letter from Aubry he had despatched them to spy on the meeting between Delestraint and Hardy in order that they might point them out to the *Abwehr* who would then arrest them. The letter, of course, had used only cover names – 'Didot' (Hardy) and 'Vidal' (Delestraint) – so the job of Multon and Moog was to be at the métro station to see if they recognised any Resistance faces. If they did, then the chances were that they would belong to whoever 'Didot' and 'Vidal' were.

Hardy and Multon vaguely knew each other and nodded a greeting as they boarded the train. Though Multon knew Hardy was connected with the Resistance, he did not, of course, know that he was the wanted 'Didot'. Spy and counter-spy went to their adjoining sleeping-cars as the train pulled out of Perrache station. At 1 a.m. it halted at Chalon-au-Saône and Moog, alerted by Multon, got off to warn the German police that a known Resistance man was aboard. Hardy was arrested, as was the unfortunate Vichy official who was sharing his compartment, and the two men were placed in a prison cell in Challon.

On 10 June – the day after Delestraint was successfully identified and arrested – Barbie travelled to Chalon to interrogate Hardy. Then he took him to Gestapo HQ in Lyon where, eight hours later, he was released unharmed.

The damning new evidence created a sensation. Hardy had never once mentioned to his Resistance comrades that he had been arrested. That, and the fact that Barbie had quickly released him without harming him, seemed sinister pointers to the conclusion that Hardy had done a deal to save his own neck. Equally damning was the evidence that when Hardy met Aubry on Sunday, 20 June, 1943 to discuss the following day's meeting at Caluire, Aubry arrived at the riverside rendezvous to find Hardy sitting next to a man whose face was hidden in a newspaper. Aubry beckoned Hardy away so that they could talk alone. It was later discovered that the man on the bench had been Klaus Barbie.

A second trial was convened for Hardy. Though he admitted he had lied at the first trial, the proceedings ended in a hung jury and he was freed. He later made a name for himself as a Hollywood screenwriter, adapting his own book *'Bitter Victory'* into a film starring Richard Burton, Curt Jurgens and Ruth Roman. After a broken marriage, and weighed down by the unending burden of suspicion, he became a recluse, drifting from lodgings to lodgings, living off the royalties of a series of books, the overriding theme of which was the moral dilemma involved in betraying one's friends.

In the 1970s, safe in South America, Barbie gave several newspaper interviews. Inevitably the Hardy affair figured prominently in each of them. Barbie maintained that the railway saboteur had co-operated fully with him after his arrest at Chalon; that he had told him the time and general location of the Caluire meeting and had even left yellow chalk marks to guide the Gestapo to Dr Dugougon's villa. 'I didn't even hit him,' he said. 'In fact we sat together and drank cognac.'

It sounds conclusive. But Barbie is an inveterate liar and braggart, a highly political animal, well aware of his capacity, even today, to cause mischief in France. In other interviews, for example, he claimed that Jean Moulin was handed over unharmed to the Vichy authorities, or, alternatively, that he committed suicide. A third version was that he had been betrayed by the Gaullists because they had discovered that he was a crypto-Communist.

Hardy maintains that the traitor was Henri Aubry. 'He betrayed Moulin because of ambition or because he was stupid.' he told me. 'At my trial I could see him sweating as he gave evidence, in fear that the truth would come out.'

A wartime British agent to whom I spoke in Paris believes that a woman double-agent was the betrayer. Others say a Gestapo man overheard an indiscreet reference to the Caluire meeting by Aubry when he lunched with three friends in a Lyon restaurant.

Even the undeniable fact that Hardy was arrested and released unharmed by Barbie is not in itself conclusive proof of his guilt, for on several occasions the Gestapo chief used just this technique to sow dissent and suspicion in the ranks of the Resistance.

Barbie claims I was the betrayer, but Barbie could not tell the truth if he tried [says Hardy]. He hated France and still hates her. He will do anything to throw mud at France. And at his trial – do you think he will confess to his crimes and say sorry?

The truth of that meeting at Caluire is that we were all Boy Scouts, playing at war. Everyone knew of the meeting. There were loads of indiscretions. Yet they point the finger at me, saying I was not handcuffed because Barbie had agreed to my escape. Nonsense ... I was not handcuffed because he had not brought enough handcuffs to go round. When they were taking us outside, I spotted a gap and, like any rugby player, knew how to exploit it, so I put my head down and ran.

I was lucky, though I took a bullet in my arm. Some people even say I shot myself to make it look real. Can you credit such crazy talk?

No, the facts are quite simple. At the end of the war the Resistance wanted a sacrificial lamb to atone for Moulin's death. I was that lamb.

The old man shuffles with me to the door of the cottage and shakes hands. Before I leave he tells me of an extraordinary journey he made to Bolivia in 1972 to confront Barbie, the man who, in one way or another, has been the architect of his ruined, bitter life. The French journalist who accompanied him and paid his expenses engineered a meeting in the street between the two men. Hardy begged Barbie finally to lift the weight of suspicion from his shoulders. The Nazi merely smiled and walked off.

Innocent or guilty, I ask, what is it like to live under such a heavy burden for so many years?

'It is like being a cuckolded husband. Every day the pointing fingers and the whispers behind your back. It hurts, but one lives with it. Now I am dying and soon, I suppose, I shall be dead.

'Then it won't matter any more.'

Chapter 5

THE INNOCENTS

White under their dusting of snow, the distant lofty peaks of the Jura Mountains stand as a backcloth to the rumpled green carpet of the valley and foothills. Clinging to a hilltop, an old church stands sentinel to the hamlet of Izieu-Ain.

Below, nestling in a fold of the hills, stands a grey house, four-square and solid, its shutters a faded green above window-boxes where ranks of red daisies dip and bob in the breeze. Above them on the wall is a plaque of carved stone, all the names and ages of the children of Izieu — the youngest 3, the oldest 13.

But they are all long dead and there is little more than the stone plaque and a few grieving memories to mark their short span of life. Their physical remains are nothing more than grey mud at the bottom of a Polish pond.

From this beautiful corner of France they were taken by Klaus Barbie and sent on a journey that took them to a marshy place close by the forest of Birkenwald. It took its name from that of the nearest village, Oświęcim.

Which, in German, is Auschwitz.

Auschwitz was not a single camp but part of a sprawling complex of factories and camps called Birkenau-Auschwitz. Several well-known German firms, among them DAW and Siemens and Krupp, had premises in the complex where slave labour was forced to work for the Nazi war machine. In that respect it was similar to many of the twenty concentration camps which had been built mainly on German soil, to house Hitler's enemies.

Birkenau was what made it different, for that part of the

complex existed solely for the extermination of those the Nazis deemed to be undesirable – Jews, Poles, Czechs, gypsies, homosexuals and mental defectives. It was, quite simply, a death factory whose five chimneys belched flames and smoke for twenty-four hours a day as the corpses of men, women and children were burned.

Deportees from all over Europe would arrive, packed like cattle into railway-trucks which would clatter to a halt at the sidings and disgorge their terrified and bewildered passengers. Often they had travelled for days with little food or water and no sanitary arrangements; many, particularly the very young and very old, died *en route*. Others had slipped over the edge into madness.

Even those who had retained their sanity must have doubted their reason as they dropped from the cattle-cars, for their first sight was that of the camp 'orchestra' playing to welcome them. Gaunt and starving, shabby in their blue and white striped prison suits, there was something surreal about their music, usually jaunty ragtime, at this infamous railway junction with its coils of barbed wire, armed SS guards and batteries of powerful arc-lamps beneath which savage dogs patrolled.

As the dazed newcomers were bullied and jostled into line the camp medical officer, Dr Josef Mengele* and his assistant, Dr Fritz Klein, would pass slowly down the ranks. Mengele, oblivious to the music of the orchestra, would whistle Wagner constantly as he strolled along the line, pointing to each person in turn and directing them to one of two queues. Those sent to the right were the healthy adults and older children whom he deemed fit enough for slavery in Auschwitz, where only the most strong and determined would survive more than a few months of the backbreaking

*Dr Mengele, a graduate of Frankfurt and Munich universities, used Auschwitz inmates as human guinea-pigs for agonising and usually fatal medical experiments. After the war he escaped through Italy to South America. In 1973 he became a naturalised citizen of Paraguay where he still lives under the protection of that country's government.

labour and the savagery of the guards. Those whom
Mengele, the 'Angel of Death', waved to the left were the
children up to the age of 12, the elderly, the sick and the
lame. Their destination was Birkenau.

Daily the wretched musicians of the orchestra were forced
to play their cheery music as they witnessed the familiar
harrowing scenes as families were cold-bloodedly split up.
Small children would cry for their parents as the guards
shoved them into separate queues. The anguish of their
mothers and fathers was tempered only by the belief –
cynically fostered by the guards – that their offspring and
ageing relatives would be taken to another part of the camp
where they would be cared for without being forced into the
rigours of hard labour.

The Germans went to extraordinary lengths to maintain
this charade, for they knew that if the newcomers learned
the real fate of their infants and elderly parents – a choking
death in the gas chambers – there was a good chance that,
notwithstanding guns, clubs and dogs, they would rise and
attack the guards. So ambulances with red crosses were
provided for the feeble and the sick who would be solicitous-
ly helped aboard by SS men; trucks would draw up to transport the rest. And at Birkenau the long columns of men,
women and children would be marched off to the gas
chambers, clutching soap and towels, believing that they
were to take a showerbath to clean up after their appalling
journey. Specially picked SS men, smiling and jolly, would
accompany them on that last walk to extinction, often
taking the trusting hand of an infant and joking with him on
the way to the gas chambers.

Even inside the huge chambers the ghastly subterfuge was
maintained, for shower heads projected from the ceilings.
But no water sprayed down on the upturned, waiting faces.
The door would slam shut and there would be a pause of
several minutes as the operators waited for the body heat to
raise the temperature by a few degrees, thus ensuring that
the gas would spread more effectively. In the ceiling was a

glass panel over metal latticework. When the time came an SS guard wearing a gas-mask would open the panel and release a cylinder of Zyklon-B, a gas with a base of hydrate of cyanide, developed from a commercial rat poison.

Death took only a few minutes. The first to die were the children, for the heavy gas would sink to the floor before rising slowly to engulf them. In terror they would begin to scream, clinging to the legs of their parents or other adults. The more they screamed, the faster they inhaled the gas. . . .

When all sounds of life had ceased, the gas would be vented off and the pile of corpses dragged out with the use of special hooked poles. Often a handful would still be alive, but they, too, went the way of the dead – into the roaring flames of the crematory ovens. The men who carried out this work were themselves prisoners, known as *Sonderkommando*, forced to their task at gunpoint. Those who refused would be horribly beaten before being shoved into the gas chamber with the next consignment to be liquidated.

Many went mad, particularly those who had to push their own wives, children and parents into the chambers and then fling their bodies into the ovens. For them it must have come as a blessed relief when the time arrived, as it did every three or four months, for they themselves to be herded into the 'showers' when their successors as new *Sonderkommando* took over.

On a busy day or if the SS guards grew impatient, the smaller children and the toddlers would be separated from the rest. Then, without the 'benefit' of gassing, they would be flung, wild-eyed and shrieking, into the flames. . . .

On the morning of Thursday, 6 April 1944 the children of Izieu were at their lessons in the big house. They had lived there for almost a year, forty-one Jewish youngsters sent there in great secrecy from all over France by parents who feared for their offspring's lives in that harvest time for the Final Solution. So remote and well-hidden was the house, far from German eyes, that they felt sure their sons and

daughters would be safe there even if they themselves were
to be rounded up for deportation. They had packed small
suitcases with clothes and a few cherished toys and sent
them off to the sanctuary at Izieu where ten adult volunteers
would care for the children until these insane times had
passed.

But someone had told Barbie about Izieu. Similar houses
were dotted all over France. Local SS commanders knew of
their existence but chose to turn a blind eye. Not, however,
Barbie; not for him even this rare mercy. Jews were Jews
whether they were infants or not, and orders were orders.

On that morning in early spring the first warning was the
whining of engines in low gear as a convoy of trucks and
vans wound its way up the hill and bumped along the drive-
way into the courtyard in front of the house. Tailboards
clattered down, doors slammed and the sound of running
jack-boots rang out over the quiet hillside as Barbie's men,
weapons at the ready, surrounded the building.

The white-faced staff – five men and five women – were
dragged out into the courtyard and held at gunpoint while
storm-troops and French *milice* searched the house
systematically and drove the children out to join them.
Barbie gave the order to load the vehicles and there were
wails of fear as the armed men grabbed the youngsters.

'I was working in a nearby field when I heard the commotion and walked over to investigate,' recalled Julien
Favet, a farmworker in his sixties who still lives in Izieu.

It was horrible to watch – the Germans just flung the
children, even the tiny ones, into the back of the vehicles
as if they were just so many sacks of rubbish.

One of the SS jabbed me with his gun and forced me
towards the back of a van, but his chief – later I was to
realise he was Barbie – saw what had happened and
came over and shouted at the man.

Then he began yelling at me and dragged me out of the
way, saying 'Get out of here and clear off!' I was only too

glad to escape, but my heart went out to those poor children who were crying in their fear and pain. Long after the trucks had vanished from sight round a bend in the road I could hear them sobbing and screaming.

That evening, at 8.10, well-pleased with his day's work and looking forward to a leisurely dinner, Barbie signed a signal to the head of the Gestapo in Paris:

IN THE EARLY HOURS OF THIS MORNING THE JEWISH CHILDREN'S HOME 'COLONIE ENFANT' AT IZIEU-AIN WAS RAIDED. IN TOTAL 41 CHILDREN AGED FROM 3–13 WERE TAKEN. FURTHERMORE THE ENTIRE JEWISH STAFF OF 10, 5 OF THEM FEMALES, WAS ARRESTED. CASH AND OTHER ASSETS WERE NOT TAKEN. TRANSPORTATION TO DRANCY FOLLOWS ON 7.4.44. – BARBIE.

As the Gestapo chief dined in style at the Lapin Blanc, the staff of the 'Colonie Enfant' sought to comfort the terrified children, nursing the smaller ones and reassuring the older ones with smiles and lies. Next morning they and their forty-one charges were pushed aboard a train and sent to Drancy.

No single place in France, except Vichy itself, is more symbolic of the shame and dishonour of the country under German occupation than Drancy, a dingy, run-down suburb on the north-eastern fringes of Paris near Le Bourget airport, where, in August 1941, the Pétain government had established an internment camp. A huge half-finished apartment and factory complex, Drancy was to spend the rest of the war as the antechamber to Auschwitz.

All but twelve of the seventy-nine trains that carried the Jews of France to annihilation clanked off on their long journey to Poland from the sidings near Drancy. More than 70,000 people passed through its gates and, except for a pitiful few, this was the last they saw of France. And yet, from the day it opened until the day it was liberated by the Allies, Drancy was guarded by Frenchmen, *gendarmes* in their familiar cloaks and blue and white képis. Camp commandants were drawn from the upper echelons of the French police service. Searches, selections for deportation and the loading of the trains were supervised by officials of the Commissariat Général aux Questions Juives (CGQJ), a department of the French civil service.

From the outset there were protracted wrangles between the bureaucrats as to who was in charge of Drancy. The Prefect of Police, Admiral François Bard, was happy to provide guards but declared that it was the responsibility of the Prefect of the Seine, Charles Magny, to supply food, bedding and other necessities. Magny protested he had no funds for such purposes and maintained that these supplies were a police problem.

While they argued, conditions in Drancy deteriorated. Within months of its opening, dysentery was rife as the undernourished internees attempted to subsist on a steady diet of cabbage soup which wrought havoc with overworked bowels. In desperation the French called in a sanitary team from the German medical corps who, according to a contemporary French intelligence report, 'raised hell' and ordered more than a thousand sick internees released.

The report went on:

> Those who have not with their own eyes seen some of those released from Drancy can have only the faintest idea of the wretched state of internees in this camp which is unique in history. It is said that the notorious camp of Dachau is nothing in comparison with Drancy.

By July 1943 the Germans had so tired of French ineptitude at the camp that they took charge of the central administration. A staff of five SS men were placed under the command of *Hauptsturmführer* Alois Brunner*, an experienced Final Solution administrator fresh from Salonika where he had helped murder Greek Jews with exemplary efficiency. Though *gendarmes* continued to provide the guards and the CGQJ helped shuffle the paperwork, Drancy, from that moment, became a German responsibility . . . as did all Jewish affairs throughout France.

It is a tragic and ironic comment on the way the French ran Drancy that under the murderous Brunner rations and conditions in the camp actually improved!

Improvement, however, is a relative term. When the children of Izieu climbed off the train and marched into the camp they found themselves in conditions of unspeakable discomfort and squalor with thousands of other children and adults. One of the latter, Georges Wellers, describes what life was like for them:

> The children were in bare rooms in groups of one hundred. Buckets for toilet purposes were placed on the landings because many of them could not walk down the long and inconvenient stairways to the toilets.
>
> The little ones, unable to go alone, would wait agonisingly for help from female volunteers or another child. This was the time of the cabbage soup at Drancy. This soup wasn't bad, but it was hardly suited for children's digestion. Very quickly all the children suffered from acute diarrhoea.
>
> They soiled their clothing, they soiled the mattresses on which they spent night and day. With no soap, dirty underclothing was rinsed in cold water and the child, almost naked, waited for his underclothes to dry. A few hours later, a new accident and the whole process had to be repeated.

*Brunner, one of Eichmann's loyal subordinates, was personally responsible for thousands of deaths in Greece and Czechoslovakia. He still lives under Arab protection in Damascus, Syria, where he is known as 'Dr Fischer'.

The very young ones often didn't know their names, and then one had to ask their friends who sometimes gave some information. Family and first names then being established; these were inscribed on little wooden dog-tags.

Every night one heard the perpetual crying of desperate children from the other side of the camp, and from time to time the distraught calling-out and wailing of children who had lost all control.

For twelve weeks the majority of the children from Izieu suffered at Drancy. On Friday, 30 June – three weeks after the heady news of the D-Day landings in Normandy – they were loaded into railway-trucks and shipped to Auschwitz.

When they got there the orchestra was playing and Dr Mengele told them to go to stand in the queue on the left, so they did as they were told and wondered why their teachers and a few of their older brothers and sisters had to join the other queue. Then they marched up the hill with the men in the black uniforms who smiled at them and gave them soap and towels so they could have a shower . . . up the hill to the big building which had fire and smoke coming out of its chimneys and which the men in black said was a bakery. . . . A few hours later their ashes were raked over in the ovens as the weary, half-crazed *Sonderkommando* toiled to keep up the production quota under the whips, kicks and curses of the SS, while their teachers and the older children were marched into a slavery which not one of them survived.

That month, between 1–26 July, 442,000 men, women and children were slaughtered in the gas chambers of Birkenau and went up the five chimneys in rolling clouds of thick, black smoke. The figures were an improvement on those for May – 360,000 – but something of a shortfall when compared with June's 512,000 . . . a total of 1,314,000 in the space of less than three months.

Each night the roaring flames from the 'bakery' chimneys lit up the skies as the sweating *Sonderkommando* toiled like zombies to burn the never-ending column of corpses, raking out the tons of grey ash that threatened to choke the ovens. Later this was tipped into a pond behind the camp or cast on to the waters of the River Vistula.

Even in death the Jews served their Nazi tormentors. Their possessions and clothing were seized, rings were cut from fingers, gold teeth wrenched from dead jaws, hair shaved for mattress stuffing, body fats clarified to make soap – an obscene industry to fuel a lunatic's war that was all but lost.

And while the lunatic in Berlin moved towards his personal *Götterdämmerung*, the men and women he had infected with his madness eased up not one jot in their cruelty and barbarism as they herded the Jews of Europe into the Holocaust.

Among the children snatched from Izieu by Barbie were three brothers of the Benguigi family – Jacques (13), Richard (6) and Jean-Claude (5), who were sent to Drancy for only a week before leaving for Auschwitz on Thursday, 13 April 1944. When they arrived their mother had already suffered there for eleven months, a victim of Mengele's medical experiments in the infamous Block 10. Only one thought sustained her and gave her the strength to fight against the agony and degradation – the knowledge that her three young sons were safe and well at the Izieu hideaway. Clinging fiercely to life, she prayed for the day when the pain and suffering would end and she would be reunited with the boys. She survived, though pitifully incapacitated by Mengele's surgical butchery.

Her body might have come through Auschwitz but a part of her died on a spring day in 1944 when, in an engulfing moment of horror, she recognised Jacques's sweater in a pile of clothing that had belonged to recently gassed prisoners. Mme Benguigi knew that Jacques would never have left Richard and Jean-Claude; therefore they, too, must have been arrested and deported. If he, 13 years old and fit to work, had been murdered, then there was no hope for the little ones. Demented with grief, she cursed the men who had slaughtered her children and swore vengeance on them. Half a lifetime later her chance was to come when she played her own part in helping to bring Klaus Barbie, the man who had sent her children on the road to Birkenau, to justice. . . .

On the same train which transported the Benguigi brothers from Drancy to Auschwitz was Edith Klebinder, a former governess to a Parisian family. At 31 she was the same age as Barbie, whose men arrested her in Lyon on Monday, 20 March 1944 for the crime of being Jewish.

Because of her race Edith could no longer work as a governess and the only job she could find was as an office cleaner in the headquarters of the UGIF (Union Générale des Israélites de France), situated near Lyon townhall. (The UGIF was the body set up by France's Commissioner-General for Jewish affairs to absorb all the charities and social agencies created by the Jews, thus creating one body representing Jewry. Every city and large town had a UGIF office, a sort of clearing-house manned by Jews through which French – and later German – racial edicts were passed on to the Jewish population.)

At her flat in Vaulx-en-Velin, a Lyon suburb, I met Edith Klebinder in the spring of 1983, soon after her seventieth birthday, a small, bright woman whose iron spirit brought her safely through the miseries of Auschwitz. As we talked in the communal garden of the apartment complex, two small children broke off their game to stare curiously at the number – 78675 – tattooed on her right forearm.

'I got that at Auschwitz,' she told me. She went on:

We were to the Germans like cattle . . . creatures to be given numbers rather than the dignity of a name. I was tattooed on my first day in the camp.

We had arrived the night before and wondered what sort of a place it was because we found an orchestra playing and thin people, like skeletons, dancing in time to the music. That was a Saturday – 15 April – after two terrible days during which we had been jammed in the cattle-train from Drancy – sixty to each truck. Some had died, others had become gibbering idiots.

It was twilight when we arrived, but there were powerful lights all around and an SS officer strode along the train asking at each wagon if anyone spoke French and German. I said I did. He told me to climb down and ask everyone's age. From outside the wagon I could see in the distance flames lighting up the sky which I assumed came from some sort of rubbish incinerator.

I began asking people's ages and the officer followed me, organising them into two separate queues. . . .

So, unwittingly, Edith aided the Germans in their murderous selection of victims.

I suppose it was about two weeks later that I finally discovered the true use of the 'incinerator'. I had gone to the infirmary to visit the sick people who had been on my train, only to find it was empty, everyone had gone. By this time I had been told that the flames came from the bakery; when I asked about the sick who had been sent to the infirmary I was told the truth about the 'bakery'.

My ears heard, but my brain could not believe. We were used to the brutality of the guards, but surely even they – young Germans with parents and children of their own – could not bring themselves to exterminate infants and old people?

I soon learned that they could. After a few weeks in the camp I found I could instantly recognise those newcomers who would be put to work and those who would be sent to the 'bakery' at Birkenau. But we who knew were not allowed near the new arrivals; could not warn them . . . even if we could have got word to them they wouldn't have believed us; would have thought us insane.

So day after day we were forced to watch through the fence as the play-acting went on – the guards smiling and pretending to be friendly as they herded the little ones and the old people, carrying their towels and soap, towards the gas chambers.

One day in June we were watching another party of poor devils on their way to their deaths when a Hungarian woman who was with us suddenly screamed: 'Oh, dear God – there are my two children and my mother!' She had been in the camp long enough to know where they were heading, so she ran to an SS officer and threw herself at his feet in the mud of the compound.

She begged him: 'Please, Herr Offizier – I am working for you, but I will work even harder, I will do anything you want, if you will save my children and my mother. I will feed them and take care of them, they will be no trouble. Please, in the name of God, save them.'

The officer gave a cynical smile and said: 'You are wasting your time. At this moment they are already smoke going up the chimneys.' Then he walked away and left her sobbing with grief in the mud. The poor girl lost her mind; just one of the many whose reason was destroyed by Auschwitz.

Barbie and the men like him who sent her and countless others to almost certain death in the camps are just as guilty as the guards who actually carried out the killings. Barbie knew what was in store for those he sent to Drancy to wait their turn before going to Auschwitz.

He should be made to pay for his crimes. I don't believe in killing people. If he were executed we would be doing the same to him as he did to us.

But he must spend the rest of his life in prison so that every day that is left to him he can contemplate and reflect on the terrible misery, grief and pain he had brought to so many people.

'And you,' she said to me, as we strolled in the spring sunshine, 'you must write your book and tell of the things that Barbie has done. Tell everyone about the camps and the

little children marching to their deaths. Most of all, tell it to
the young who do not believe me when I tell them.

'They must understand, for only when they do can we be
sure that such things will never again happen.'

It is Wednesday, 20 July 1983 and Lyon is hot and sunny.
The legal system that is working to bring Klaus Barbie to
trial is grinding forward in slow French fashion. A middle-
aged Frenchwoman in sandals, tinted glasses and a summer
dress emerges into the sunlight from the greystone bulk of St
Joseph's Prison, close by Lyon's Perrache station. Mme
Simone Lagrange is 52. Despite the warmth of the day she
shivers slightly and tells of the meeting, only minutes before,
with Barbie.

'He looked so mild at first,' she says, 'and then he started
staring at me. The eyes were the same – cruel, metallic, they
never left my face. His gaze made me feel almost physically
ill.'

Then she tells how Barbie, whom she had gone to identify
formally, eyed her up and down in the presence of prosecution and defence lawyers before bursting out laughing:
'Why, madame, I am in jail and I haven't seen a pretty
woman in a long time.' And with that contemptuous, lascivi-
ous stare the years rolled back to 1944 when Mme Lagrange
was Simone Kadousche, a 13-year-old schoolgirl:

When we reached Gestapo headquarters we were put in a
room on the fourth floor where I saw Barbie for the first
time. He came towards my parents and me, stroking a big
grey cat and, without raising his voice, he asked my
mother if I was her only child.

Mama replied that she had two younger children, but
she didn't know where they were. Then Barbie, who had
paid no attention to my father, came over to me and
politely asked where my two little brothers were.

When I told him I did not know, he gently set the cat
on the table, then struck me brutally hard twice, saying

he could find them well enough himself.

The German woman who was our keeper advised Mama to tell him where my brothers were if she wanted to escape interrogation, but Mama and I knew we were going to be sent to a concentration camp where little children were killed.

On 7 June they came to take me to Place Bellecour where Barbie himself was waiting to question me again. He said politely that if I told him where my brothers were he would send all three of us to an old folk's home where we would be well taken care of and not deported.

After I told him again that I did not know, he came over to me, grabbed me by my long hair and yanked me close to him. Then he struck me over and over again for at least fifteen minutes. I was in great pain, but did not want to cry. Finally he let me go and I fell on the floor. He kicked me in the stomach until I got up again. He, himself, took me to jail. He told my mother that she had no heart to allow her daughter to be beaten, and if she would talk now, he would stop interrogating me. Then he struck her several times.

I was taken back to the Gestapo four times, but you can be sure they got nothing out of me. They put me in a different cell and I didn't see Mama again until 23 June 1944, when we were shipped to Drancy before being sent to Auschwitz where Mama was burned on 23 August 1944. My father was killed on 19 January 1945 as the camp was being evacuated.

Many years later, in an interview in South America, Barbie expounded his continuing faith in the Nazi creed. 'I am an SS,' he said. 'Do you know what it is to be an SS? 'It's to be a fighter whose forebears have been vetted for four generations back before he is granted the honour of joining. It's to be a professional – chosen by Hitler himself.'

It is a strange 'honour' that makes a man send children to die in choking swirls of cyanide gas; an odd kind of 'fighter' whose only fighting was against unarmed civilians. The term 'professional' sits uneasily on the shoulders of a man whose career was so marked by corruption.

In Paris I met Alexandre Halaunbrenner, the owner of a sportswear shop, who related to me yet another example of Barbie's 'honour':

> In 1943 our family consisted of my father Jakob, my mother Itta, my older brother, Leon (13), my three sisters, Mina (8), Claudine (4) and Monique (3). Between 1941 and 1943 we were interned in several camps in the southern zone, but by August 1943 we were living, under surveillance, in our house in Lyon.
>
> We were living at 14 rue Pierre-Loti in Villeurbanne when the Gestapo came to our house at 11 a.m. on 24 October 1943. There were three of them. Two were tall and about 40 years old; the third, who was much younger, was plainly in command. He waited impatiently for the arrival of my father's nephew, who must have been betrayed to the Gestapo and who was eventually arrested and killed by them in 1944.
>
> While my little sisters were clinging to my father, the younger man pulled out his revolver, terrifying us. His face has haunted me ever since. When I saw Barbie's picture in a magazine in 1971 I recognised him at once, as did my mother.
>
> My brother Leon, who was tall for his age, came home about 6 p.m. The Gestapo men had been at our home all day, one of them watching outside the door. When my brother arrived, they searched him and took him away along with our father. My mother began to scream in Yiddish for them to let my brother go and we all wept and howled, but in vain. Barbie shoved my mother aside as she was trying to yank her son and her husband back, took out his revolver again and beat her hands with it to make her let go.
>
> We waited all the next day in the street for the two who

had been arrested to return, my sisters clinging to my mother's skirts. Then we saw a German Army truck stop in front of our house, probably to take us away. Pretending to be passers-by, we moved on down the street leaving everything behind.

A few weeks later, on 14 December, we learned from a Jewish friend that our father had died 'in the hospital'. I went with my mother through all the city's hospitals, but we could not locate him. Then I thought of going to the morgue — and there we found my father. He had been there for three weeks. He had been shot in a summary execution at Gestapo headquarters. Seventeen machine-gun bullets were in his neck and chest.

My brother, Leon, was deported and died of exhaustion from labour in the Polish salt mines after eight months. My two younger sisters, Mina and Claudine, were put into the Jewish children's camp at Izieu where we thought they would be safe, but Barbie did not spare them when he liquidated that refuge in April 1944. My sisters were deported on 30 June 1944 and were murdered when they reached Auschwitz.

After speaking to Alexandre, I met his mother. Itta Halaunbrenner wept for her lost children as we talked in the basement of Alexandre's shop. Had they lived, Leon would be in his fifties and the two girls in their forties. But to Itta they will be forever little ones, youngsters she thinks of every day in what has become a lifetime of mourning.

Tears streamed unchecked down the lined face as she told the story of the destruction of her family. When I asked, finally, what Barbie's fate should be, a look of pure anguish crossed her features. Fighting to control her wavering voice, she told me: 'That man, that Barbie — he should be made to spend the rest of his life with me so he can see every day how I suffer and how I cry for my little ones. He should suffer and cry with me, every day until I die. Only then will my pain and grief cease.'

Time and again Barbie's 'honour' as a 'fighter' brought him into contact with children, often Jewish, and never once, it seems, did his feelings as a father prevent him subjecting them to appalling brutality.

I remember one day Barbie had two young Jewish children in his office, a brother and sister, from whom he was trying to discover the whereabouts of the rest of the family [recalls Fuchs, the interpreter]. They wouldn't talk, though, because every Jewish kid had been warned about the camps. The Chief was cajoling them – he could be pleasant and kindly-looking when he wanted – but he wasn't fooling them at all and they refused to say anything.

Suddenly, in typical fashion, he lost his temper and went wild. He picked up the younger child, the girl, and holding her by the ankles, smashed her head against the office wall with a terrific swing. Then he threw her body aside and grabbed her terrified brother, yelling at him to say where his family was. The boy couldn't speak, but just shook his head.

Barbie went berserk and killed the boy in the same manner. I suppose he was about a year older than his sister who looked to me about 11 or 12.

On another occasion I was at my desk in the École Santé Militaire when I heard an uproar at the top of the stairs and saw a very pretty teenage girl, little more than a schoolgirl, trying to get away from Barbie. Her clothing was all disarranged and she was terribly distressed. Barbie was red in the face and breathing heavily. He grabbed her and began hitting her, calling for the guards.

Two SS men appeared and dragged her back to Barbie's office, sobbing her heart out.

God alone knows what happened to her.

Chapter 6

DEFEAT

On Sunday, 3 September 1944 – exactly five years to the day after war broke out – a handful of American jeeps picked their way carefully across the damaged Wilson bridge over the Rhône and nosed into the battered heart of Lyon. The capital of Resistance was liberated.

The beginning of the end for the German occupiers had dawned on Tuesday, 15 August when the United States Seventh Army and Free French forces had stormed the beaches of the Côte d'Azur near Cannes in a seaborne landing from the Mediterranean, only to find that the invasion was virtually unopposed.

The opposition consisted of the 11th Panzer Division and this rapidly fell back, retreating northward up the Rhône Valley towards Lyon. Along every yard they were harried and chivvied by Resistance fighters whose build-up of parachuted arms during four years of Occupation had given them a considerable punch as a guerrilla force. Fighting alongside the Americans during the first nine days, they helped destroy 1,500 German vehicles, kill more than 1,000 troops and take some 3,000 prisoners.

Since D-Day on 6 June German losses had been staggering: 1,200,000 dead, wounded and missing, seventy-eight divisions destroyed and almost a quarter of a million troops trapped in pockets in France. Hitler's 'Thousand-Year Reich' was crumbling.

By Monday, 28 August the Allies had cleared the Rhône Valley and the road to Lyon was open. To all intents and purposes the German 19th Army had ceased to be a fighting force and, by 2 September, it had withdrawn from the city to retreat towards the Fatherland.

In those final, chaotic days Barbie prepared to flee, but
before he did so he had to 'clean up the mess', as he later
admitted to American interrogators. First there were the
records, all the incriminating files and dossiers containing
details of Gestapo atrocities, which had to be destroyed.
Then he set about systematically eliminating those who
knew too much – more than a score of collaborators and
informers who had once been of invaluable help to him, but
who would now undoubtedly collaborate with the new
authorities. Their testimony could hang him. Not surprisingly they were hunted down and shot with brutal efficiency.
Among them was his regular girlfriend, a ravishing dark-
haired Frenchwoman whose many nights of passion in
Barbie's bed bought her no reprieve. She was shot with the
others.

The bloody fight by the now-unified Resistance groups did
much to speed the German evacuation and to redress four
years of shameful French collaboration. Their victory was
the gallant Jean Moulin's legacy to his country.

But in Lyon there was another legacy ... the Barbie
legacy.

Klaus Barbie's reputation as the Butcher was one which he
relished, enjoying the power it gave him and the fear it
engendered in others. He was, after all, a lower-middle-class
provincial of mediocre education who, in normal circumstances, would aspire to nothing more than a fairly hum-
drum occupation and existence. Yet thanks to the war he
had become a commissioned officer, once the almost
exclusive province of the sons of the aristocracy; an officer,
furthermore, in the elite SS, the Führer's own Praetorian
guard. He had a smart and impressive uniform in which to
swagger and a rank, albeit junior, to attach to his name.

He was still only 29 years old when posted to Lyon, yet
was put in a position of immense power – literally that of life
and death – and had access to huge sums of money which he

used unashamedly for his own creature comforts and to buy himself a reputation in the security service.

If he had qualms about his actions in Lyon, he never showed it. In his own eyes he was simply a soldier obeying orders, and in this respect the Barbies of the world are not unique to Germany; they abound in the KGB and other secret police organisations in every country where the power of the State is allowed to override human decency and individual rights. But the catalogue of atrocities committed by the young *Obersturmführer* while he was merely 'obeying orders' during his twenty-one months in Lyon makes harrowing reading.

On Tuesday, 9 February 1943 he led a raid on the UGIF headquarters in rue Sainte-Catherine, rounded up eighty-six staff and despatched them to Drancy. As Jews their fate was inevitable; they were shipped to Auschwitz from which few, if any, returned alive.

Less than a month later, on Monday 1 March, German troops surrounded a block of houses in Villeurbanne, an industrial suburb to the east of Lyon, and herded 1,000 residents into the street for classification. Some 150 were detailed off and marched to a waiting cattle-train.

When Paul Chabert, Mayor of Villeurbanne, asked Barbie their destination he was told they were going to Compiègne, an internment camp north of Paris that served a similar purpose to Drancy. The mayor protested; the men had been dragged from their homes almost naked, the weather was cold and throughout the long journey the trucks would be unheated. After the war Mayor Chabert recalled the incident:

> We asked Barbie for permission to go to Compiègne to take food and clothing to the unfortunate prisoners. Finally he granted it ... but when we arrived the commander of the camp told us: 'Lieutenant Barbie did telephone me that you were coming, but he definitely instructed me to forbid you to see the prisoners.'

Some time later we learned that the men had been deported to Germany. Only thirty came back.

Retired police superintendent Adrien Richard, who still lives in Lyon, saw at first hand the sickening results of Barbie's methods on Monday, 10 January 1944, in the cellars of the by-then infamous École Santé Militaire.

I learned of a round-up by the Germans on quai Sainte-Claire following the deaths of two German policemen who had been killed in circumstances the police did not solve.

About 1 a.m. the following morning I received a telephone call at my house asking me to accompany my divisional superintendant to Gestapo headquarters for a purpose about which I was not told.

When we got there a German officer tried to explain that prisoners had been executed because, he alleged, they had revolted. On this occasion we did not see Barbie, though he was head of the department, but an officer asked us to follow two NCOs to the cellar to identify the corpses. They led the way and two others followed us. All four were armed with sub-machine guns.

As we got into the cellar corridor we were overpowered by the unmistakable odour of warm blood. We went further along and came across a puddle of congealed blood in front of a cell door.

The door was opened by one of the NCOs and we witnessed a frightful spectacle . . . corpses were piled up in a corner of the cell and literally swimming in a sea of blood.

They were all young men who had been killed by machine-guns as they faced the door. They were stuck together or half-stretched out, and I remember that one of them, a postman still in his uniform, had half hoisted himself out of his seat before being killed. His face was stretched in a rictus grin.

We then realised that the officer's explanation – that

they had been killed during an act of revolt — was not true. The position of the corpses made it impossible.

It is highly unlikely that any of the men had been involved in the death of the two German policemen, yet Barbie rounded them up at random and ordered them to be murdered. Their feelings of incomprehension in the last moments of their lives can only be imagined. And the grief of wives, children and parents when their husbands, fathers and sons did not return home is why, even today, the people of Lyon spit out the name of Barbie like a curse.

The sweeping expanse of place Bellecour is at the very heart of Lyon, a huge and stately square, dominated by a fine equestrian statue of Louis XIV and flanked by trees beneath whose branches the flea market gathers each Saturday. On the north side of the square, facing Louis's statue, in a recess on the corner of rue Gasparin, is an altogether more modern monument, a carving in relief below which there are always vases of fresh flowers.

This is the city's memorial to five more innocent victims of Barbie's murderous rule. In 1944 this corner plot was a café, Le Moulin à Vent, a popular bar which had been requisitioned by German officers and police, though members of the public were still allowed to make use of its facilities. Few, other than prostitutes and those Lyonnaise who worked for the Germans, chose to exercise this privilege.

Around midnight on Wednesday, 26 July a bomb exploded in the café, causing considerable damage but injuring no one. When Barbie heard of the attack he flew into a rage, vowing vengeance on the Resistance.

Next morning, minutes before noon, a *Wehrmacht* lorry drew to a halt in front of the Moulin à Vent and a posse of soldiers, armed with rifles and sub-machine-guns vaulted over the tailboard. They stopped all the traffic in the street and cleared a stretch of pavement of pedestrians. A hush fell over the square and as a nearby clock began to chime twelve the apprehensive crowd heard the sound of a car speeding over La Guillotière bridge and into rue de la Barre from the direction of Fort Montluc.

It pulled to a halt behind the army lorry, a grey car which many recognised as one of the several used by Barbie. The nearside door swung open and a young bareheaded man was bundled out. The waiting soldiers aimed their guns and a volley of shots sent the man jerking and spinning down on to the pavement. Another young man was propelled out of the door . . . and another . . . a fourth and a fifth . . . each to be cut down in the chattering gunfire.

The Gestapo car had stopped for only two or three minutes. When it roared off round the square, followed by the army truck, all five men were dead − four lay sprawled across the pavement, the fifth was in the roadway with his head lolling in the bloodied gutter. All day, until long after nightfall, the corpses lay in the summer sun, swathed in flies, while distraught relatives awaited German permission to remove them. Only when Barbie judged that the brutal message had been absorbed by the townsfolk did he give his approval for undertakers to be called.

Among the stunned witnesses in the crowded square was British agent, Arthur 'Tommy' Thompson. For years he had been the representative of the Singer Sewing Machine Company in the South of France and he spoke perfect, effortless French. In the early days of the Occupation he had been recruited by the Secret Service and given the RAF rank of flight-lieutenant. He had spent the war on intelligence-gathering operations around Lyon. Today he still lives there, running a small engineering company. We met in a hotel close by the place Bellecour and he gave me his account of the event.

Those young fellows were gunned down without mercy. Yet they were totally innocent − hostages who had been arrested in June and therefore could not possibly have had anything to do with the café bombing.

But that was Barbie's style. Innocent or guilty he couldn't care less ... all the bastard cared about was his reputation as a man to be feared.

I often used to see him around the town; he was a familiar figure, sometimes in uniform and jack-boots, but most times in civvies, always well dressed and rather debonair-looking. On occasions he'd be in a car or a jeep, but the rest of the time he enjoyed striding down the streets as if he was daring people to have a go at him.

But no one ever did. The whole city was terrified of him. He knew it and rejoiced in the fact.

As the tide of war inexorably turned against the Germans, the capital of Resistance became the capital of oppression, with Barbie wielding ruthless power like some medieval warlord.

At the behest of his master, Eichmann, Barbie despatched trainload after tragic trainload of deportees on the harrowing journeys that inevitably fetched up at the five blazing chimneys of Birkenau-Auschwitz. Many hundreds were not even given the slender chance of surviving Auschwitz's slavery; they were tortured to death or gunned down indiscriminately in an ever-worsening orgy of 'reprisals' against the work of the Resistance known as the Maquis. Women, children, priests and nuns – at various times all fell victim to the Butcher.

On Thursday, 29 June 1944, 724 men were deported to Germany as slaves. Three days later, thirty-three women suffered the same fate. Another fifty-five men and women followed them on 22 July. Ten trains crammed with deportees left Lyon at the beginning of August. In June 122 prisoners were massacred in the surrounding districts, and a total of 100 on 8, 12 and 19 July.

On Saturday, 26 August in Villeurbanne a group of young patriots, by then actively fighting the Germans, erected a barrier in place de la Bascule. Within minutes a German patrol had surrounded a block of houses which they set on fire. As residents tried to escape from the flames the soldiers opened up with their guns, driving them back into the inferno. Eight people were killed and three injured.

The same day an armoured car and a lorry loaded with soldiers were driving along the quai du Rhône near Pasteur bridge when there was the sharp crack of an explosion. Without seeking to investigate the cause the Germans immediately mounted an attack on one of the houses on the quay, blasting away the front door with an anti-tank gun, which started a bad fire in the hallway. The inhabitants took refuge in the cellars; the besiegers shouted to them that they would be spared if they quitted the building. As they left, unarmed and groping through the billowing smoke, the troops opened fire, killing five people.

There had been no attack on the Germans. The 'explosion' was merely the sound of a car tyre bursting.

At around the same time the Bron military airfield in east Lyon was being heavily bombed by the US Army Air Force. A total of 109 of Barbie's Montluc prisoners – two-thirds of them Jews – were driven to the air base and forced to fill in bomb craters on the runways. When the task was completed, seventy-three of them were herded to the brink of an unfilled crater and machine-gunned by the Germans. The remaining thirty-six were also murdered – but this time the killers were their fellow-Frenchmen, members of the *milice*.

Even worse was to follow. On Sunday, 20 August, as the advancing Allied troops marched towards the city, Barbie gave orders that 110 men and women were to be called out 'without baggage' from Montluc. Only too aware of the significance of that ominous phrase, the prisoners marched out and were driven to the village of Saint-Genis-Laval a few miles south of the city. Among them were the Abbé Larue, Professor of Science at the Lazarists' College, and Canon Boursier, vicar of Sainte-Thérèse de l'Enfant Jésus, Villeurbanne.

When they arrived, the prisoners, who were handcuffed

together, some in pairs, others in fives, were prodded into the guardhouse of the disused Fort Côte-Lorette. It was 6.30 p.m. Minutes later the residents of Saint-Genis-Laval heard the abrupt clatter of small-arms fire echoing round the fort, repeated bursts that continued sporadically for three-quarters of an hour as groups of prisoners were systematically slaughtered.

The killings took place on the first floor while the next group of victims was held at gunpoint on the ground floor. When a batch had been shot the executioners would call down the stairs for another party to be sent up. The man who ordered them upstairs was Max Payot, a member of the *milice*. Later he was to testify: 'After some time the prisoners had to walk over a heap of their former comrades and by then blood was pouring through the ceiling.'

Three prisoners managed to make a break for freedom through the ground-floor window of the guardhouse, dodging a hail of fire from German soldiers and plain-clothed French auxiliaries. Two were recaptured and shot instantly, their bodes flung on to ever-growing pile of corpses. The third contrived to get away, though he was wounded in the knee.

When the last man was dead and the guns fell silent, the soldiers brought jerry-cans of petrol from their lorries and soaked the bodies, walls and floors. A grenade was tossed in through the door and the fort erupted into a huge funeral pyre. At 10.45 p.m., by which time the building was an inferno from end to end, the convoys of German and *milice* vehicles roared out of the village and turned north for Lyon. Within minutes Saint-Genis-Laval was rocked by a series of explosions that continued to rip the fort apart for several hours as relays of delayed-action bombs detonated to scatter and destroy the evidence of the massacre.

Two days later Cardinal Pierre Gerlier, Archbishop of Lyon, Primate of the Gauls, and a loyal supporter of Marshal Pétain, returned pale and shaken from visiting the scene of the atrocity. He wrote later:

It was with horror I witnessed some of the bodies being discovered. I can still see the painful effort made by some young men to separate two great blocks of wall, and I can still hear the sudden cry of one of them: 'Here's one!' while he dragged from between the two enormous stones human remains whose precise nature it was almost impossible to determine.

It was a fairly large piece of bone; from half of it the flesh had entirely gone, while a sort of stump of burnt flesh adhered to the other half, the whole being covered with red and black earth. A little way off, a bare skull was uncovered and then a few other indefinable fragments of human bodies.

The pieces were gathered together and, in a big room nearby, were added to the lamentable series of other discoveries made in similar circumstances.

There was a certain number of coffins. In each of them had been assembled the pieces that appeared to belong to the same body. For many of them there were merely large sheets of paper on the floor. On these, bones and fragments of flesh as well as bits of earth, on which there were traces of blood, were gathered.

After praying in this charnel house while the macabre jigsaw puzzle was slowly assembled, the cardinal drove back to his palace and wrote an angry letter to Knab, Barbie's commanding officer, which he handed over in person:

Monsieur le commandeur,
I have just returned from Saint-Genis-Laval and it is my painful duty to make to you, while expressing the indignation I felt at a sight for which I can find no words, a solemn protest against the abominable cruelty of the executions carried out there on 20 August and which follow, alas, on many others no less horrible.

How sad it is to think of the hatred deeds such as this are bound to arouse at a time when the world is pathetically trying to find its way back to fraternity and peace.

I am 64 years of age, Monsieur le Commandeur, I went through the 1914 war and have seen during the course of my life, which has been very varied, many horrible sights. I have never seen one which revolted me so much as that which I saw just now.

Even if one could prove that all the unfortunate people executed the day before yesterday were malefactors – and no one can say they were – I would still assert that it was unworthy of a Christian civilisation, or even a human one, to put them to death in such a manner. What can one say, therefore, when no wrongdoing can be imputed to them?

If these words seem to you excessive, Monsieur le Commandeur, go in person to see what has happened. I cannot believe that your human heart will not be appalled by it, as mine was, and those of all the witnesses of these horrors.

I am persuaded that you are personally ignorant of the refinements of savagery which marked the atrocious execution. But I have no hesitation in saying that those who were responsible for it are forever dishonoured in the eyes of humanity. May God forgive them.

It is unlikely that such righteous anger had any effect on Knab; even less likely was it to stir the conscience of Barbie in his determination to turn Lyon into a bloodbath in the remaining days, fast running out, of German rule.

The only response to Gerlier's letter was a reply from Barbie which began, respectfully enough, 'Eminence . . .' but then went on to tell him, in effect, to mind his own business.

The cardinal's attitude towards the Germans and the collaborationist government of Vichy was, throughout the Occupation, somewhat ambivalent. Though he was no Nazi, he was a staunch Pétainist who was rather too inclined to 'render unto Caesar'. Like most French clerics he made little

or no demur when the *Statut des Juifs* was proclaimed, but
he did begin to protest when the Jewish deportations began.
It is to the credit of his flock that many Jewish children were
hidden from Barbie's hunters in Catholic homes and religious houses. When the regional prefect of Lyons, Alexandre
Angéli, demanded to know the whereabouts of the fugitive
children, Gerlier himself refused to give the information.

If Gerlier's forthright letter to Knab had no effect, there
was one from Yves Farges, a leading Resistance figure,
which produced dramatic results. Posted in Lyons on 21
August, the day after the Saint-Genis-Laval killings, copies
were sent to Prefect Angéli, the president of the Red Cross
and the Swedish consul. The letter, whose contents Farges
said should be passed to Knab, announced that the Maquis
had captured a total of 752 German prisoners in the Haute-
Savoie region. Of these, eighty had been executed in reprisal
for Barbie's latest atrocity. The remainder would be considered, henceforth, not as prisoners but as hostages to be
shot in retaliation for any further German mass executions.

Uncharacteristically, Werner Knab ordered a stay of
execution for those Resistance fighters among the 950
prisoners who remained in Montluc. For the Jews in his
custody, however, there was no such reprieve. Even as
American armour battled through the southern approaches
to Lyon, Barbie ordered forty of them to be liquidated. Less
than two weeks earlier, on Friday, 11 August, he had despatched the last deportation train to leave French soil —
direct to Auschwitz. Aboard were 308 men, women and
children, most of whom perished in the gas chambers of
Birkenau during the five months before the victorious Red
Army liberated that obscene corner of a Polish forest.

While Lyon continued to reel under this sustained campaign
of institutionalised, officially sanctioned repression and
violence on the orders of Himmler and Eichmann, Klaus
Barbie never once let up on his own personal taste for
torture and terror. To be in a situation where he was face to

face with the person he was tormenting, afforded him a perverted satisfaction he could never achieve in the mass, setpiece security operations against the partisans or the Jews.

> If he thought he was losing face or being made a fool of, if he thought someone was defying him or refusing to be forced into submission, then his mood would change violently and he would become an enraged monster, [says Gottlieb Fuchs].* Then all he could think of doing was to hurt people in the most appalling way he could dream up. God help the victim because he could expect absolutely no mercy. To some Gestapo officers torture was only a means to an end ... a tool to be used to gain vital information. To Barbie, torture was an end in itself; often I got the impression he wasn't particularly interested in getting the information ... only in enjoying the pleasure that hurting people gave him.

To this end the École Santé Militaire was furbished with a series of sophisticated torture chambers, some in the cellars, others on the fourth floor. Most were equipped with two baths, one filled with scalding hot water, the other with cold, into which prisoners undergoing interrogation would be alternately and agonisingly ducked to the point of neardrowning. Each room had a table with leather straps to which victims could be pinioned while his inquisitors burned him with hot irons, electrical probes or, on occasions when a prisoner was particularly close-mouthed, with the flame of

*The interpreter was arrested, without Barbie's knowledge, on 20 December 1943 by Gestapo men who had photographed him passing information to agents of the Swiss Secret Service. When he was taken to the École Santé Militaire for questioning, an angry Barbie ordered them to remove his handcuffs before marching into Knab's office to speak on his behalf. When his efforts to sway Knab failed, he returned to Fuchs, shook his hand and said: 'Well, you're going to have to pay the price – but well played.' Fuchs spent two years in various concentration camps and was liberated from Belsen in 1945.

an acetylene torch applied to the soles of the feet. Near at hand were a variety of truncheons, iron bars, whips and thin chains used for beating 'clients' into bloody submission. An added refinement was the provision of hypodermic syringes for injecting drugs or corrosive acids into vital organs.

Barbie's enthusiastic acolyte in these ghastly rituals was François André, a French Nazi whose terrifyingly deformed features, the result of a motor accident, had earned him the nickname *Gueule Tordue* ('Twisted Face'). One of his favourite instruments of torture was a spiked ball attached to a steel cosh by a chain, rather like a smaller version of a medieval knight's flail. Its capacity for inflicting unbearable pain and permanent, crippling, injuries made it one of the most terrible weapons in the Barbie armoury.

In March 1944 a Resistance worker called Lisa Lesèvere was arrested and found to be in possession of photographs that were to be used for false papers for Maquis members. She was also carrying a letter addressed to 'Didier', a low-ranking member of the Resistance. At that time Barbie was hunting Albert 'Didier' Chambonnet, an important regional Resistance chief whom the Gestapo had been seeking for more than a year.

The *Obersturmführer*, mistakenly convinced that Lisa knew the whereabouts of the more important 'Didier', took personal charge of the case. He opened the interrogation by beating up the young woman and, when this had no effect, summoned four others, including *Gueule Tordue*, to help him. They hung her from the ceiling by her wrists and beat her with coshes and wooden clubs. Next day they stripped her and, after a severe beating, held her down in a bath of water until she passed out. Revived by a doctor, she came round to find Barbie and his cronies laughing and offering her a drink of wine.

She was tortured for almost three weeks during which her resolve to say nothing hardened. She refused to speak even when *Gueule Tordue* tied her face down to a chair and savagely beat her with his spiked flail. His blows smashed her spinal column, leaving her permanently disabled. Mercifully she fainted. When she recovered consciousness she found herself in the middle of a strange, surrealistic scene. There was the sound of Chopin's 'L'Héroique' being played on a piano ... a glimpse of a young girl's ankles ... and Barbie's face only inches away from her own.

His voice was quiet and soothing as he stroked her hands. 'What you have done is magnificent, *chérie*. Nobody has held out as long as you have. It's nearly over now. I am very upset, but we must finish. Go on – make a little effort. Who is "Didier"?' Stubbornly the girl shook her head and almost passed out again as Barbie rained angry blows on her face, screaming: 'I don't want to see this stupid woman any more. Get rid of her!' Lisa saw the rest of the war out, crippled with pain, in Ravensbruck concentration camp north of Berlin.

An earlier victim, Resistance fighter Maurice Boudet, who was arrested in July 1943, recalls: 'Barbie was a monster. He always had a cosh in his hand. When I was unconscious, he pushed me into the freezing bath. Then the cosh again, and acid injected into my bladder. He really enjoyed other people's suffering.'

André Frossard was stripped by Barbie and his wrists were lashed to his ankles. Like a trussed chicken on a spit, a stout wooden dowel was pushed beneath his arms and he was carried to the bath: 'It was like an axle around which they turned me, dragging me by the hair.' The choking Frossard almost drowned several times as Barbie held his head underwater. When he fainted he was kicked back into consciousness.

For Josef Touitou, a Lyon Jew, the nightmares recurred on the day Klaus Barbie returned to the city as a prisoner. Touitou, by then 53, began once again to scream in his sleep as the former Gestapo chief languished in Montluc, the fortress where, as a teenager, Josef had been locked up with his parents, ten brothers and a baby sister.

I was taken to his office at Gestapo headquarters where Barbie questioned me about my family and friends, wanting to know if they were in the Resistance. He was cold and clinical and, at first, questioned me a lot, but then seemed to forget me.

His secretary [Thedy Scheffer] was kind to me because I was so young. She often gave me sweets when her boss wasn't looking.

Barbie personally tortured young Josef on several occasions and his victim still cannot bring himself to describe what happened. When asked for details his hands with their deformed fingers (his nails were pulled out at Auschwitz) start to flutter uncontrollably and he becomes visibly distressed.

His wife Esther has, however, managed to piece together some of the horrors that were inflicted on her husband.

To this day he is terrified of chains and of fire. The sound of chains sends him quite mad because, at some stage, they beat him with chains. He can't bear a hot or a cold bath because they tortured him by pushing him from one to the other and holding him under the water. He shudders when he sees striped clothes because they remind him of the prisoners' uniforms at Auschwitz and cannot stand the sound of screaming, even though he himself screams in his sleep.

When I first met him (in Algeria after the war) he was like a wild animal, sick yet aggressive. He had poured acid on the number the Nazis had tattooed on his arm, he couldn't walk and had suffered a complete nervous breakdown.

Josef Touitou was the only member of his family to survive. His parents, ten brothers and baby sister had all gone to fuel the ovens of Birkenau.

Never a day goes by that I don't think of the beloved family that Barbie destroyed [he says, fighting back tears].

Words cannot convey the hatred I feel for this creature.

I am afraid I would not be able to control myself if I came face to face with him in the courtroom. I have tried to forget, to wipe out the terrible memories. I don't attend the meetings that some former internees hold and I always avoid that part of the city where the Gestapo headquarters were situated.

But I can't forget. I would like to kill Barbie and would be prepared to spend the rest of my life in prison for doing it. But he won't suffer, not like I and thousands of others are still suffering ... but the world must know what he did so that it can never, never happen again.

Sometimes the mere threat of torture was enough for Barbie's victims. In Lyon the story of a prisoner flinging himself out of a third-floor window at the Hôtel Terminus in an attempt to kill himself to avoid further agonies still persists. The man was, in fact, Alfred Newton, an Englishman, who with his brother Henry, operated in Lyon as an agent of SOE (Special Operations Executive). They were betrayed and arrested by Barbie in April 1943 and, according to their own accounts, were savagely tortured by him — to such an extent that Alfred made his unsuccessful suicide bid. He was saved — though suffering a broken leg and a fractured shoulder — because the Germans had had the foresight to string a safety net across the hotel courtyard. The brothers were sent to Buchenwald where they survived the war and returned to England. Such were the privations they endured in the camp, however, that they were broken in body and spirit and died after years of terrible sickness.

They were undoubtedly brave men, but those French Resistance fighters arrested with them insist to this day that neither man suffered physical torture at Barbie's hands. They maintain that Barbie's lavishly-detailed descriptions of what lay in store for them were sufficient to cause Alfred's suicide attempt and to provoke a confession from Henry.

André Courvoisier, an SOE radio operator who was imprisoned in Montluc claims: 'There was never a mark on Henry.' A female agent who travelled with him on the train when the Gestapo transported the brothers from Lyon to Paris is also adamant that Henry was never tortured. Barbie himself, in an interview given in South America, said: 'He was surprisingly easy to break. He confessed immediately and revealed a Resistance camp near Grenoble.'

Whatever the truth of the matter, it is a fact that on Monday, 5 April, 1943, the day following the arrest of the Newton brothers, Barbie and a Gestapo squad turned up at Le Puy and arrested four of their Resistance contacts who were awaiting the arrival of parachuted supplies.

It would be presumptuous of anyone who has never faced torture and the threat of death to pass judgement on brave men whose courage may have momentarily wavered at a time when they were frightened and lonely; the story of the Newtons is recounted here not to condemn them, but rather to illustrate Barbie's fearsome reputation. It was a reputation based on almost two years of unremitting cruelty, during which the city of Lyon learned that their Gestapo chief would never be swayed by any flicker of morality, compassion or humanity in his pursuit of his Führer's mad goals.

Barbie's rule of Lyon lasted for 657 days, ending with his escape as the Americans battled their way through the suburbs towards the city centre. And when, on 3 September 1944, liberation came, when the gates of Montluc were swung open by singing partisans, when the few remaining wretches were freed from the Hôtel Terminus then it was time to count the cost.

Those 657 days had seen 4,000 executions, more than 7,000 deportations, and pain, grief and fear on a scale impossible to calculate – a monstrous butcher's bill for one provincial city.

Chapter 7

GÖTTERDÄMMERUNG

Forty years on, the scars that Klaus Barbie and others like him inflicted on the enslaved nations of Europe are still plain to see. They are the misshapen fingers of men whose nails were ripped out with pliers; the shuffling steps of a broken inmate of Auschwitz or Belsen; the cries of those who still wake screaming in the night; the tears of old women who weep for long-dead children.

All this and more Barbie bequeathed to the people of Lyon, but he also left them something less tangible . . . the guilt which his web of corruption created. It lasts to this day, for beneath the surface of Lyonnaise life everyone knows that his collaborators still live in their midst. Many were shot or hanged after the liberation, but others who were more successful in covering their tracks remain, pillars of society and venerated as Resistance heroes.

For them Barbie's presence as a prisoner is a ticking time-bomb. One former Resistance man told me:

> I and many like me hope that at Barbie's trial he will stand up and name names. For the last forty years there have been men and women here growing fat on the proceeds of their treachery. We do not know who they are, though everyone has his own suspicions, but we do know they must now be trembling at the prospect of exposure. It is good that they should suffer; because of them thousands of their neighbours suffered. Now, at last, it is their turn.

Barbie served his masters well during the war; now he has his one and only chance to serve France by helping finally weed out those who have tarnished her name for so long.

Despite his constant talk of SS 'honour' and his carefully nurtured image of a devoted and obedient National Socialist, Barbie indulged in corruption to an extent that would have horrified his puritanical Führer, constantly diverting funds from the Reich treasury for his own use. Money and valuables looted from Jews and other detainees were used to finance not just his ring of French collaborators but also his own taste for expensive suits, flashy women and black-market food. Gottlieb Fuchs, tells how the Chief, with a wary eye to the future, used to keep in his safe considerable reserves of cash in the currency of many different countries, among them several hundred English pounds – his insurance fund in case Germany lost the war. Nor was Himmler's loyal lieutenant above selling his prisoners back to their families in exchange for ransom money, a crime which, if discovered, would certainly have led to his execution by decree of an SS court of honour.

In the summer of 1983 I met the remarkable Mary Lindell, an 88-year-old Englishwoman and widow of a French count. Throughout the war she lived in France as an agent of MI9, the British Secret Service branch responsible for the network through which Allied escapers were smuggled out of Occupied Europe. Her most famous 'clients' were the surviving 'Cockleshell Heroes' – Royal Marines who had used flimsy canoes to paddle into Bordeaux harbour to attack German ships with limpet mines. Betrayed by a female member of the French Resistance, she survived Ravensbruck concentration camp and returned to France as a heroine. In 1946 she was awarded the Croix de Guerre to go with the one she had won in 1916 as a Red Cross nurse. From the British government came the Order of the British Empire.

She and her husband, the Comte de Milleville, had three children, two sons and a daughter, with whom Mary lived in

Lyon. The younger son, Octavius, was arrested for Resistance activities and deported to Mauthausen concentration camp in Austria where he died in the notorious stone quarry in which prisoners were forced to labour.

Her older son, Maurice, like his mother, was an MI9 agent, active in directing escaping Allied airmen along the various escape routes. In 1942 he was arrested after being betrayed by one of Barbie's French collaborators who had approached him, posing as a Resistance man anxious to reach England. He was taken to the Hôtel Terminus where he was savagely beaten by Barbie's aides until, as he commented: 'I looked like strawberry jam.' He was coshed repeatedly on the back of the head with rubber truncheons, receiving eye injuries which have left him permanently short-sighted. When he refused to talk, he was flung into a prison van and carted off to Fort Montluc.

Mary Lindell recalled the incident when we spoke in her Paris apartment:

Maurice had made an ass of himself by being caught in the way he had been. Barbie was a bastard whose reputation I knew well, so I didn't give much for my son's chances in his hands and decided to try to get him out of prison before they really started on him.

My daughter, who has since died, was a beautiful girl, a real stunner. She was in her late teens and she knew Klaus Barbie ... in what way I did not know, nor did I ask. But she knew him and I asked her to see him and ask how much money he would take to arrange Maurice's release.

She came back with a message from Barbie saying that he wanted 40,000 francs. I was delighted to hear it; I would have been willing to pay much more. But I didn't trust the bastard an inch, so I gathered the banknotes together, took a pair of scissors and cut them all in two. One half I hid, the other half I gave to my daughter to deliver to Barbie. I told her to tell him that he would receive the missing portions of the notes only when he had safely delivered Maurice to a friend's house near place Bellecour.

Barbie kept his side of the bargain. Maurice was taken to the house and allowed to go free. Only then did my daughter hand over the missing parts of the banknotes.

Another of the strange coincidences that litter the story of the Butcher of Lyon lies in the name of Mary's daughter, the beautiful teenage go-between who mixed in the same circles as the Gestapo chief.

Her name was Barbie.

In the early days of the Nazi police state, when Himmler's black-clad empire was tightening its stranglehold on the Reich, one of his staff with a taste for the histrionic coined the phrase *Nacht und Nebel*. Literally 'Night and Fog', it came to symbolise the absolute power of the State to spirit into the shadows all those who would not walk with Adolf Hitler in the dawning light of the Nazi era.

Countless thousands vanished into the limbo of *Nacht und Nebel*. One night a husband, son or brother would be about his normal business; the next he would have disappeared, often never to be seen again. There would be no charges, no trial, no appeal and, in most cases, no clue about his fate, not even a body for grieving relatives to bury. This knowledge that the police could come at any time and, totally untrammelled by the restrictions of law, torture and murder in accordance with their own whims was a powerful psychological deterrent to those who might have felt tempted to oppose the cause of National Socialism.

Barbie exploited the technique to great effect and, when the time came, used it not as a weapon against others but as a camouflage for his own quiet fading from the scene of his crimes. Despite his posturing as a Nazi idealist, he was a realist, entertaining no illusions about the eventual fate of the Third Reich and those who, like himself, had served it with

such slavish barbarity. Even when Field-Marshal von Rundstedt's brilliant counter-attack in the Ardennes during the
winter of 1944 – the Battle of the Bulge – temporarily
restored Hitler's flagging fortunes, Barbie recognised that
defeat was inevitable.

From then on the smokescreen of his own personal version
of *Nacht und Nebel* began to shadow his movements. The
once-flamboyant '*Chef*' became an increasingly cloudy
figure as the darkness of confusion and the fog of war closed
around him. Almost forty years afterwards it is difficult to
pierce the gloom since only occasional glimpses of the man,
these often confusing and contradictory, remain.

He quitted Lyon during the final days of August 1944,
probably a week before it was liberated by the Americans,
making his way through the chaos and devastation to
Germany where, it is believed, he visited Regina and Ute in
Trier. One version of his whereabouts during the last days of
the German occupation of France, however, describes how
he received foot wounds from an exploding grenade during
his 'clean-up' of Lyon when he massacred his one-time collaborators and informers. As a result he was hospitalised in
the Black Forest before being sent to Halberstadt for rest
and recuperation.

If this is true, then his treatment and convalescence were
brief indeed, for another report places him in Holland on
Thursday, 7 September, there to inflict a second tragedy on
the family that had yielded him his most celebrated victim
apart from Jean Moulin. Hermannus van Tongeren, Grand
Master of Holland's National Order of Freemasonry, had
been arrested by Barbie in October 1940. Five months later
he died in Sachsenhausen concentration camp.

Since that time his son, Hermannus junior, had striven to
keep the craft of Freemasonry alive in the face of Nazi
persecution of its adherents. He had also become involved
with the ever-growing Dutch Resistance, allowing its
members to use a room in his house at Heemstede to monitor
BBC news bulletins and to operate an illegal printing press.

On 7 September three Germans arrived at the house and demanded to be shown round. They were, they claimed, surveying the property to judge its suitability for possible requisitioning by the German authorities. Although the 44-year-old businessman suspected that the 'survey' was a fabrication he had little option other than to invite them in. His suspicions hardened to certainty when one of them, ignoring the ground-floor accommodation, went straight upstairs and made unerringly for the door of the first-floor room used by the Resistance.

There was no doubt that he had been betrayed. The Germans knew what they were looking for and searched with methodical patience until they found it – a hidden bundle of Resistance pamphlets awaiting distribution.

Van Tongeren was interrogated for seven hours. Then one of his captors confronted him with a fresh discovery which he had found secreted in the room: a banned book about Freemasonry. The German flipped it open and riffled through the pages until he came to a head-and-shoulders illustration of the Grand Master of the National Order of Freemasonry.

'Do you know this man?' he asked mockingly. 'Is he perhaps a relative of yours?'

'Yes – I am his son,' van Tongeren answered quietly. 'I, too, am a Freemason and I am proud of it.'

'In that case, there is someone from the SS in Amsterdam who would very much like to meet you,' responded the German, tossing the book on to the table and reaching for the telephone.

Hermannus's sister, Charlotta, recalls what happened next:

Three more Germans drove to Heemstede from Amsterdam to collect my brother from their colleagues who had questioned him, first at his home, then in his office where they had gone to make a further search.

The actual arrest was made at his office, after which

they dragged him out to a car, whose back windows were covered with drawn curtains, and set off for Amsterdam.

Somewhere on the Heemstede — Amsterdam road, when the car was travelling at high speed, they opened one of the back doors and flung my brother out. He hit the road and rolled over many times, receiving severe injuries, yet somehow he managed to stagger to his feet. The car braked to a halt and the three Gestapo men ran back with guns in their hands, opening fire on Hermannus. He went down, terribly wounded with bullets in his neck and through one lung. Then they drove off, leaving him for dead.

He lived, in fact, for thirty hours, during which time he managed to relate to his wife what had happened to him. He told her: 'I recognised them, those three men in the car. They were Barbie, Kempin and Kalb.' He later became unconscious and died.

Barbie, Kempin and Kalb — the same trio that had arrested Hermannus's father in October 1940 — had been briefly reunited to strike another blow against Dutch Freemasonry and to bring fresh grief to the van Tongerens. Charlotta remembered only too well the bitterly prophetic warning her father had whispered to her '*Watch out for the one called Barbie . . . he's the most dangerous one of them all. . . .*'

Barbie had been rewarded for the older Tongeren's capture by promotion being elevated within a month to the rank of *Obersturmführer*. Now, once more, the misfortunes of the desolated van Tongeren family proved to be a stepping stone. Within a week of Hermannus's death, Barbie was recommended for promotion to *Hauptsturmführer* (Captain). The recommendation, dated 14 September, was written by his superior, *Sturmbannführer* (Major) Wanninger at the headquarters of the RSHA, the *Reichssicherheitshauptamt* (Reich Central Security Department) in Berlin, and it read:

Barbie is known at headquarters as an enthusiastic SS leader. He has a marked talent for discovering information and for the pursuit of crime. His most meritorious accomplishment has been the clearing out of numerous enemy organisations. The *Reichsführer*-SS Himmler has expressed his appreciation to Barbie in a personal letter commending him for his pursuit of crime and his untiring action in the struggle against the Resistance.

From the point of view of ideology and character, Barbie is a sound man. Since his training and during his employ in the SD, Barbie has pursued a regular career as a director of the 'superior service' and, providing there is no objection to his promotion, it is proposed that he be advanced, from 9 November, 1944, from the rank of SS-*Obersturmführer* to that of *Hauptsturmführer*.

Was his promotion to captain a reward for returning to the Netherlands to strike another blow against the Freemasons? Or did it come, while he was recovering from grenade wounds, simply because of his length of service?

David Barnouw, a historian with the *Rijkinstituut voor Oorlogsdocumentatie* (the Dutch Institute of War Records) in Amsterdam, who helped with my research into the Nazi occupation of Holland and Gestapo operations there, was unable to discover a single reference in his voluminous files to Barbie's presence in the country after he left Amsterdam in the spring of 1942 pending posting to Gex.

Yet Charlotta van Tongeren is adamant that it was Barbie who led the team which gunned down her brother; the same trio who had robbed her of her father. Could old age and muddled memories have played her false? That seems unlikely, for though she was 81 years of age and a resident of an old people's home when she recounted the story, her mind was sharp, her narrative precise, logical and unshakeable. At the same time it seems strange that no record should exist either in Barbie's personal SS files, of which I have copies, or in the official Dutch archives, of a second posting to Holland.

A possible answer to the contradiction may be found in Barbie's next known whereabouts – a posting to SD headquarters in Dortmund dating from 20 November 1944. Dortmund lies in the heart of north-west Germany's Ruhr, within easy driving distance of the Dutch border. So it is not inconceivable that Barbie was given the second van Tongeren assignment while waiting to take up his duties in Dortmund. Such a temporary attachment would not necessitate his being officially posted to the Gestapo staff in Amsterdam, a possible explanation of the lack of documentation.

Support for Charlotta's insistence that Barbie was her brother's murderer came when, during a visit to Amsterdam, I talked to Henk de Ruijter, a journalist with the leading Dutch newspaper *Algemeen Dagblad* who had been assigned to cover the Barbie affair after the German's expulsion from Bolivia. By coincidence de Ruijter had only recently interviewed a former member of the Resistance, Johannes Pieter Krijgsman, who was in no doubt about Barbie's reappearance in Holland.

On Friday, 3 November 1944, Krijgsman was arrested by the SD near Rotterdam and taken to Gestapo HQ in Amsterdam where he was kept and exhaustively interrogated, though not tortured, for ten days. At the end of the period he had divulged nothing about the Resistance and was taken to prison. For three months he was locked in a cell where he learned to his dismay that every man of his twenty-strong Resistance group, based at Dan Helder, had been captured by the Nazis.

Krijgsman, now 73 years old, recounted the story to de Ruijter:

It was shortly after that, in February 1945, that I came face to face with Barbie. It was a terrible experience.

I was taken from the prison to the Amsterdam offices of the Gestapo where Barbie began to interrogate me. When he found that I was not giving him the answers he wanted, he ordered his men to drag me through into another room. They they bent over me until I was stretched out on my back across a heavy table or bench, to each side of which was bolted a heavy bench vice. They grabbed my hands, forced them between each set of steel jaws and began tightening them up.

Then Barbie's questioning began. Every time I refused to answer or did not give the answer he wanted, he would punch me in the mouth. I kept losing consciousness with the pain and lost track of time completely. When they finally carted me back to my cell, three of my fingernails had been torn out by the roots and all my teeth smashed.

There can be no mistake. Barbie was the man who tortured me.

Twelve of the twenty members of Krijgsman's group were executed by the Germans. He and the rest were kept alive and subjected to ceaseless inquisitions. Why? The Germans had netted the whole group in one fell swoop so the Den Helder Resistance had ceased to exist. Any further information was, from the German point of view, largely academic. Why not shoot them all – as they were entitled to do – and have done?

Krijgsman believes he knows the answer to that question and the explanation of Barbie's return to Holland. It lay in a Resistance operation dating from over a year earlier under orders from London where the various Secret Service agencies were desperate for intelligence about Hitler's new vengeance weapons.

A German V2 rocket, forerunner of today's ballistic missile, had wandered off course after a trial firing and had fallen to earth in a remote area of northern Poland. It had carried no warhead and so was not destroyed. Though damaged by the impact, it was comparatively intact. The Germans had been unable to track down the whereabouts of their wayward missile; instead it had been found by members of the Polish Resistance who had radioed news of their find to London.

Krijgsman was given a false identity, equipped with money and forged papers, and despatched to the crash site to escort to Holland a Polish partisan who had examined the V2 and made detailed drawings of its secrets. Krijgsman crossed Germany twice, bringing back the Pole with him and handing him over to MI9 officers in Holland for smuggling across the North Sea to Britain.

On both journeys Krijgsman was helped across Germany by members of the embryonic German Resistance movement. They passed him between the Polish and Dutch borders through a series of safe houses where he was fed and cared for by anti-Hitler dissidents. Some of these gallant Germans lived in the Ruhr, right in Barbie's Dortmund 'manor' and it was *they* and not the Dutch partisans who were Barbie's quarry.

Suddenly Barbie's temporary and clandestine detachment from Dortmund to Amsterdam begins to make sense. . . .

Von Rundstedt's spirited counter-attack in the Ardennes faded in the Christmas snows of 1944 and with it died the sudden uplift of German morale it had created. Some 220,000 *Wehrmacht* troops had been sacrificed but the net result of the Battle of the Bulge was to delay the Allies by a mere six weeks.

By 16 January Hitler had shifted his war headquarters out of the path of the advancing Red Army, moving it from East Prussia to a fortified bunker beneath the Reich Chancellery in the centre of Berlin. There he was to spend the remainder of his life. Ten days later the Russians were within 120 miles of the German capital and were examining with stunned disbelief the 2,819 skeletal survivors of Auschwitz whom they had just liberated.

As Hitler raved in his bunker, hurling accusations of treachery at his generals and threatening execution to any who did not fight to the last man and the final bullet, his battered and demoralised armies withdrew into the heartland of Germany, wearily regrouping on the east bank of the natural barrier of the Rhine and waiting for the final, hope-less battle for the Reich. As they retreated they destroyed the river bridges behind them, leaving the Americans and British with the unpalatable prospect of a waterborne cross-ing of the mighty waterway under fire, an assault that would inevitably exact a heavy toll in the loss of men and equipment.

One bridge, however, remained intact – the Ludendorff rail bridge at the picturesque town of Remagen, a few miles to the south of Bad Godesberg, Barbie's birthplace. A race began with the American 9th Armoured Division striving to reach the bridge before German sappers could destroy it. On Wednesday, 7 March the Americans won, their tanks battling across the bridge at Remagen to establish an historic toehold in the heart of the Reich. A second division crossed to help consolidate the victory and from that moment all effective German resistance north of the Moselle collapsed.

In the closing months of the war, Barbie found himself with a mixed bag of last-ditch fighters at Halle – a sorry lot, soldiers, sailors, airmen, boys of the Hitler *Jugend* and the old men of the *Volksturm*, a Dad's Army of civilians too elderly for conscription. After the most rudimentary train-ing, the hapless assortment was flung into battle. Many were slaughtered. Not Barbie. As he said later: 'I took one look at them and thought to myself: I am prepared to die – but not with this lot.'

Once again he was swallowed up in the night and the fog. . . .

Though almost every German now knew that the fight was hopeless and that Germany was finished, the Gestapo continued to wield enormous power. Barbie was able to demand, and get, the necessary documents and a car for a 'special duty' trip to Berlin. There, instinctively, he homed in on Himmler's headquarters at 8 Prinz Albrechtstrasse. To most Germans it was a fearsome address; to Barbie it was a haven which, for ten years of his life, had been the hub of his world. There, surely, he reasoned, would be order, direction and calm. The *Reichsführer* would have a plan; he would tell him what to do.

But the place had gone, apart from the cellars, wiped out by the bombs which had flattened a third of the German capital. And the *Reichsführer* himself was far too busy making peace overtures to the Allies through the Red Cross to worry about the anxious, rudderless SS officers like Barbie who hung around Berlin waiting for some sort of directive.

With others Barbie drove to the Hitler bunker in Wilhelmstrasse. But there was no comfort there, either. The Führer had battened down the hatches and retreated into a fantasy world, hunching over his maps and ordering counter-attacks by divisions which had long since ceased to exist.

Demoralised and glum, the SS men found a bar that was still open and willing to serve them. After a final and somewhat hollow '*Sieg Heil*', they dispersed to work out their own salvation. A forlorn Barbie steered his car through the rubble of the once-stately Prussian capital and headed along the convoy-cluttered autobahn to the west and the Ruhr.

As the Red Army encircled Berlin, the architect of the chaos remained locked in his bunker, raging against those he believed had betrayed him. Among those he included his once-beloved Waffen-SS, the tough battlefield troops of Himmler's Black Order. In a last offensive – in Hungary – their push had collapsed in the face of overwhelming enemy superiority. In a fury Hitler ordered that four of the divisions – among them the elite 'Das Reich' and 'Adolf Hitler' – be stripped of the coveted, Gothic-lettered armbands that bore the titles of their divisions.

The Waffen-SS, who had suffered appalling losses, were incensed at this humiliation. On receiving the order one commander called his officers together and told them angrily: 'Let's take a pisspot, put all our medals in it and tie round it the armband of the "Gotz von Berlichingen" Division.' Von Berlichingen is a character in a play by Goethe who turns to one of his superiors saying 'Kiss my arse'. The Waffen-SS had finally renounced the tyrant with a vulgar gibe.

Here and there zealous pockets fought on, sacrificing themselves senselessly, but the majority of the Waffen-SS had had enough. Hitler's last hope of keeping the Russians out of Berlin, the SS 'Army Group Steiner' situated north-east of the capital, simply ignored repeated orders from the bunker for a suicidal counter-attack that would have left them facing odds of ten to one.

The ultimate proof of the SS 'villainy' reached the Führer on Saturday, 28 April when Goebbels's propaganda ministry intercepted a Reuter news dispatch recording Himmler's overtures to the Swedish Count Bernadotte of the Red Cross, which offered Germany's capitulation to Anglo-American forces in the hope of keeping the Soviet Army out of Berlin.

'A traitor must never succeed me as Führer!' Hitler thundered. Then summoning Field-Marshal Ritter von Greim, he ordered him to fly out of the beleagured city and personally arrest Himmler. In his last will and testament, he stripped the *Reichsführer* and Göring (who had also been trying to arrange peace talks) of all their ranks, titles and possessions.

From that moment on Hitler would not tolerate an SS man in his presence. On learning that his brother-in-law *Gruppenführer* (Major General) Hermann Fegelein, had been seen outside the bunker wearing civilian clothes, he ordered him to be shot in the courtyard of the Reich Chancellery.

On Monday, 30 April, ten days after his fifty-sixth birthday, Hitler and his new bride, Eva Braun, committed suicide by swallowing cyanide. They died, he in a new party uniform, she in a simple dress, lying side by side on a couch in the Reich Chancellery. Their bodies were carried into the gardens, doused in petrol and set alight. On the same day,

Goebbels and his wife also committed suicide after first murdering their six children.

Himmler, unabashed by his loss of rank and titles, continued to believe there would be a place for him in Germany's post-war administration and dreamed of forming a new Nazi party – 'the Party of National Union'. His aspirations to become Führer were eventually scaled down to the point where he declared himself willing to serve as number two to Hitler's successor, Admiral Karl Dönitz. When that offer was declined he suggested himself as Chief of Police. Finally, even the modest post of Minister-President of Schleswig-Holstein seemed adequate.

Reality finally dawned when Dönitz's short-lived rump regime collapsed and Germany's chaos worsened. In near panic Himmler prepared to escape from Berlin. Graf Schwerin von Krosigk, the Minister of Finance, warned him of his duties and responsibilities. 'It must not happen,' he said to Himmler, 'that the *Reichsführer* decks himself out with a false name and a false beard. There is no other way for you but to go to Montgomery and say "Here I am." It is then that you must assume responsibility for your men.'

Himmler, far from willing to assume responsibility for the atrocities of his men, was, in fact, planning just such a subterfuge. On Sunday, 20 May he disguised himself in a Field Security Police uniform, slipped a black patch over his left eye and pocketed identity papers in the name of Heinrich Hitzinger. With a handful of close aides he set off westwards, through Holstein and across the Elbe, in an attempt to slip through the British lines. They were captured on Wednesday, 23 May by British military policemen and, at 2 p.m. that afternoon, were handed over to No. 103 interrogation camp near Lüneberg.

The commandant, Captain Tom Selvester, noted that one of them was 'a small, miserable-looking and shabbily-dressed man'. When Selvester called him forward he removed his eye-patch and slipped on a pair of spectacles. 'His identity was at once obvious and he said "Heinrich

Himmler" in a very quiet voice.'

Military Intelligence was alerted at once and that evening Colonel Michael Murphy, head of Secret Intelligence on Field-Marshal Bernard Montgomery's staff, arrived to interrogate the prisoner. Earlier, Himmler had been searched and a phial of poison had been found hidden in his clothing. Murphy, however, was not satisfied and called for a doctor to examine the captive. When ordered Himmler obediently opened his mouth and the doctor caught a glimpse of something black between his teeth. He began to turn the SS leader's head towards the light when the jaws snapped shut with a crunch. The hidden capsule of cyanide shattered and within seconds he was dead, a victim of the same poison that had been pumped into the gas chambers of Birkenau and the other death camps.

So Himmler shared the Final Solution with his millions of victims.

In August 1945 two atom bombs destroyed the Japanese cities of Hiroshima and Nagasaki, bringing the Second World War to a cataclysmic end – and heralding the nuclear age. Hitler's thirst for power had brought about the most horrendous war the world had ever seen, killing almost 15,000,000 men in battlefields ranging over half the globe. Some 38,500,000 civilians had died too, 6,000,000 of them for no better reason than that they happened to have been born Jewish.

Few of the SS men who had carried out the genocidal onslaught on the Jews chose to follow Hitler and Himmler to Valhalla by taking their own lives. Some were caught, identified, tried and executed, but most shed their uniforms with alacrity, burned their identity and party cards and struggled desperately to melt into the chaos of war's aftermath. Few did so more assiduously than *Hauptsturmführer* Klaus Barbie.

In a post-war interview he recalled:

My war ended at Wuppertal. We turned a garage into a

stronghold. Nearby were two trucks loaded with civilian clothes for the Werewolves [those Nazis pledged to fight on after the surrender]. But no one had made any plans to continue the fight underground, probably because no one thought we would lose the war.

So I buried my gun. The four youngsters I was with and myself changed our clothes, got some false papers from the police headquarters and headed off through the forests and pastures towards the Sauerland.

They didn't get far. Only a few miles from Wuppertal, near the small town of Hohenlimburg, they ran into an American roadblock and were locked up in the local schoolhouse where they were interrogated by a former concentration camp inmate acting as interpreter for the Allies.

Barbie was a trained and experienced interrogater; his inquisitor was not. It was no even match and the Gestapo man easily convinced his captors that he and his companions were merely ordinary conscripts trying to make their way home to their families. So convincing was his story, Barbie was later to claim, that one of his jailers actually connived to help them escape by escorting them to a church near the school. 'He told us, "Go in one door and then go out of the other." We did that and then separated. That's when I began my secret life in the underground.'

Barbie set course for the south-west, heading through the war-torn Rhineland towards the Saar and Trier. There, at his mother-in-law's house, 5 Liebfrauenstrasse, he enjoyed a brief and emotional reunion with Regina and Ute, now grown to a pretty girl of five. But throughout his stay he was jumpy and on edge. He knew that as some sort of order began to emerge out of the confusion of Germany's collapse, the Allies would begin tracking down war criminals and that former SS officers would be high on their list. Though he did not consider himself a war criminal but merely a loyal officer who had carried out his duties with skill and efficiency, he was practical enough to realise that the Allies would not see him in that light.

When he received a tip-off from a former SS colleague that his name had appeared on two lists of wanted war criminals, those of the United Nations War Crimes Commission and the Central Registry of Wanted War Criminals and Security Suspects (CROWCASS), Barbie packed a suitcase, bade his family *auf Wiedersehen* and left Trier.

His destination – the small university town of Marburg – lay forty miles to the north of Frankfurt. There, he had been told, were members of the 'superior service' who would help him and who needed him . . . for work for the Fatherland.

Chapter 8

ESCAPE

On Tuesday 8 May, 1945 Germany surrendered unconditionally. It was a time of retribution. Those leading Nazis who had not contrived to escape or to kill themselves were rounded up, as were senior military figures and the men and women responsible for the infamies of the concentration camps.

For others it was a time of remorse and revulsion. The ordinary German people were forced by the Allies to visit the camps to see for themselves what had been done in their name. White-faced with shock, the adults were made to clear up the pitiful corpses and to file through the gas chambers and crematoria. 'We did not know,' they said. For many this was true; others had merely preferred not to know.

But as the scales finally fell from the eyes of millions of citizens who had once hailed Hitler as their saviour, there were others who, even in crushing defeat, plotted the revival of National Socialism – for a Fourth Reich to arise, like a Phoenix from the ashes of destruction. Among them were the men of the *Kamaradenschaft*, a brotherhood of former SS officers pledged to pursue Hitler's ideals under the command of a new Führer.

It was to this fraternity that Barbie was called when he arrived in Marburg to take up lodgings in the home of a dedicated Nazi, Robert Schmidt, at 35 Barfüsserstrasse. The pragmatic Gestapo man entertained few illusions about Nazism's resurrection and so did not share his comrades' hopeless dream. He did, however, share their penchant for intrigue and double-dealing – they had been his meat and drink for years – and he was welcomed with open arms.

In the shifting, murky waters of the underworld Barbie excelled. All the activities he had so ruthlessly suppressed in Holland and France — forgery, black-marketeering, espionage — became his way of life. Truly had the gamekeeper turned poacher. He adopted the name Hans Becker, that of a fellow-guest at Schmidt's house, thus ensuring he would have an instant cover story should he be picked up by one of the many Allied teams that were combing Europe for wanted war criminals. With an ease born of long experience he quickly acquired false papers to support this fiction.

Relieved after weeks of uncertainty to find himself with a purpose, he plunged with enthusiasm into his work with *Kamaradenschaft's* procurement organisation, the practical back-up to the policy and propaganda branches. Methodically he built up intelligence networks in the British and American zones of occupation, while raising funds for the brotherhood by means of a flourishing trade in forged papers to those who, like himself, were in search of a new identity.

His clients were almost invariably SS men, desperate to get their hands on *Wehrmacht* discharge papers that would show them to be ordinary soldiers unconnected with Himmler's death's head elite. Most of them, particularly the officers, had their own cache of funds, looted over the years from their victims, and were able to pay handsomely for their new identities. The money Barbie raised was earmarked for the eventual goal of the *Kamaradenschaft* — armed resistance against the Allied armies of occupation. When, in time, the realisation dawned that the planned guerrilla war was little more than a pipe dream, the money was put to a more practical use — that of helping hunted Nazis escape justice.

Vast sums already existed for that purpose, the proceeds of Germany's systematic pillaging of Europe, which had been spirited away by party leader Martin Bormann, who had contrived to spirit himself away at the same time. The bulk of the Reich's treasure of gold, jewels and works of art was almost certainly channelled through the highly discreet

Swiss banking system which guarantees the anonymity of a numbered account to any depositor rich enough to afford it.

Since 1945 there have been persistent rumours that some of these funds were syphoned off as generous contributions to the treasury of the Vatican, whose hierarchy maintained an enigmatic silence about the methods employed by Hitler and Mussolini before and during the war. In return Vatican diplomatic cover was granted to a handful of prominent Nazis in order that they could travel, via Spain, Italy and Denmark, to havens of refuge in South America. Subsequently the remaining millions were supposedly transferred in their wake in the form of letters of credit through a variety of multinational corporations to be used for the formation of businesses, to finance the rescue of thousands of loyal Nazis and to provide funds to maintain the international ragbag of Fascist and neo-Nazi organisations which exist to this day.

Though Barbie was a relatively small cog in the Nazi machinery at the end of the war, he may be one of the few men still alive today who know the truth of this monumental and bizarre money-laundering swindle. He may not have been far from the truth when he told his French captors in 1983 that this incriminating knowledge meant that there would be a race between many different factions to 'see who can kill me first'.

Almost daily, discreet recruiting swelled the ranks of the *Kamaradenschaft*. As it became clear that few Germans had the stomach for armed resistance and, indeed, saw their erstwhile enemies of Britain and America as the only bulwark against Russian empire-building, a new air of reality permeated *Kamaradenschaft* thinking. After all, its members reasoned, Hitler always maintained that he had not wanted war with the British or Americans and that the real enemy would always be the Communist hordes in the east. Why, then, not take advantage of the increasingly frigid Cold War and pitch in with the western Allies in their efforts to stem the spread of Bolshevism?

While his leaders agonised over the best way to pursue this course of action without getting themselves rounded up to face war crimes tribunals, Barbie managed to spend a few days in the February or March of 1946 with Regina and Ute. The result of this meeting was that on Wednesday, 11 December Frau Barbie gave birth to a son. A week later she registered the birth, naming the boy Klaus-Georg. The birth certificate – number 3008 – lists the father as Nikolaus Barbie. Many years later, Frau Barbie's truthfulness was to contribute to her husband's downfall.

Midway through her pregnancy Barbie was captured by the Americans, but escaped through a combination of luck and nerve.

Unknown to the *Kamaradenschaft* their ranks were infiltrated with double-agents, one of whom was a Swiss working for both American and British intelligence. In May he offered to approach a senior British Foreign Office official who was, he claimed, a Nazi sympathiser and wanted to know more about the comrades' proposals to help in the Cold War against the Russians. A meeting took place which seemed to augur well for this unholy alliance. However, the Foreign Office man insisted that he must have the names of prospective agents together with some indication of their possible uses before putting the SS proposals to London and Washington. Anxious to demonstrate their good faith, the *Kamaradenschaft* obliged and the trap was sprung.

Towards the end of August Barbie and an SS friend were walking in the sunshine, close to Marburg university, when a woman passenger in a cruising American Army jeep suddenly nudged the driver and pointed to Barbie. The vehicle braked sharply to a halt beside him. He recognised the passenger instantly. Her name was Erika Loos, a former Gestapo secretary whom he had known in Essen shortly before the capitulation and who, in fact, had been one of his earliest contacts with the members of the *Kamaradenschaft*.

Barbie was stunned, both by the woman's treachery and

1. Klaus Barbie:
this is the only known photograph of him in uniform.

2. The SS hierarchy:
(**a**) *left* Heinrich Himmler, head of the SS and the German police;
(**b**) *right* Walter Rauff, inventor of the mobile gas chamber.

2c. The last stages of the 'Final Solution':
the crematory ovens at Auschwitz.

3a. The grim Ecole Santé Militaire, rebuilt after American bombing in September 1944. It was Barbie's Lyon headquarters along with the Hôtel Terminus.

3b. Barbie during his days in Lyon.

4a. Gottlieb Fuchs, Barbie's Swiss interpreter, today, dressed in his concentration camp uniform.

4b. 'Max' – Jean Moulin, the leader of the French Resistance. He died at the hands of Klaus Barbie after being betrayed while attending a Resistance meeting at Caluire near Lyon.

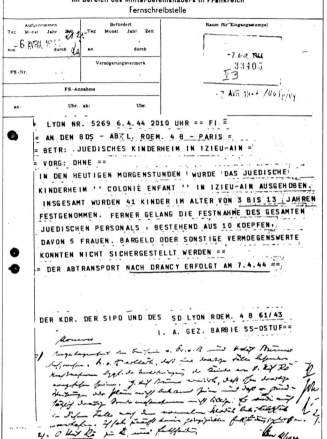

5. Barbie's signal to Gestapo HQ in Paris, informing them of his arrest of the children of Izieu. It reads: 'In the early hours of this morning the Jewish children's home "Colonie Enfant" at Izieu-Ain was raided. In total 41 children aged from 3 to 13 were taken. Furthermore, the entire Jewish staff of 10, 5 of them females, was arrested. Cash and other assets were not taken. Transportation to Drancy follows on 7.4.44 – Barbie.' (The handwritten footnotes are believed to be by Barbie.) All the children and staff died later in Auschwitz.

6a. Happier days at Izieu. The postman calls with
letters from home at the Jewish 'Colonie Enfant' in the summer of 1943.
6b. *left below* Jacques, Richard and Jean-Claude Benguigui. Taken on
Barbie's orders from the children's home at Izieu, they were to die in
the gas chambers of Auschwitz.
6c. *right below* A roadside memorial to the children of Izieu.

TOUT HOMME EST UN
MORCEAU DE CONTINENT
UNE PART DU TOUT;
LA MORT DE TOUT HOMME
ME DIMINUE, PARCE
QUE JE FAIS PARTIE
DU GENRE HUMAIN.

7a. Mary Lindell, who bribed Barbie to free her son in Lyon.

7b. Edith Klebinder, an Auschwitz survivor.

7c. Itta Halaunbrenner and her son, Alexandre. Two of her daughters died in Auschwitz after Barbie's raid on the children's home at Izieu.

8a. Beate Klarsfeld, who succeeded in getting Barbie extradited from Bolivia.

8b. Barbie, alias Klaus Altmann, in Bolivia.

by the shattering of his confident belief that he was totally unknown in Marburg. The American officer's curt 'Get in!' was reinforced by the beckoning snout of a large Colt automatic. Obediently the German clambered aboard.

In a post-war interview, Barbie recounted what happened next: 'Marburg has very narrow streets and when we reached the post office we had to slow down to let a tram pass. It was then I thought: It's now or never.'

While on standby to go to Russia in 1941 – a posting which had never materialised – he had taken a parachute course. Now the knowledge of how to fall and roll the body to avoid injury came to his aid.

'As the jeep slowed, I jumped out. There was a gasp from the pedestrians. The American looked round and in his excitement crashed into a tree.'

Sprinting as hard as he could, the tubby SS man turned into a narrow alleyway as shots rang out behind him. A bullet nicked his finger causing a superficial wound before he vaulted over a wall to seek refuge in a secluded garden:

I knocked on a door and asked the woman to hide me. She took me upstairs to a bedroom where an old woman lay in bed. I hid beneath it and heard the Americans come to the door to ask if I had passed by. The woman who'd let me in told them that she had seen me, but that I had gone on, jumping over the hedge. When they left she hid me in the pigeon coop. I stayed there until nightfall, listening to the Americans searching for me.

Urgent telex signals followed to all offices of the Counter Intelligence Corps (CIC) from its HQ in Frankfurt informing all agents that Barbie had been spotted and that he should be arrested on sight as a known war criminal.

What the CIC did not know was that the man they were hunting was – and had been for some months – an agent of the British Secret Service.

He had been recruited, probably in late 1945, by Kurt Merck, a former *Abwehr* officer who had been stationed in Paris during the war and who maintained a network of contacts through his mistress whose father had been police chief of the French capital. Merck was a valuable asset to the British espionage machine in the ever-worsening climate of the Cold War. His speciality was tracing and identifying Communist agents and agitators who, in the chaos of war's aftermath, were attempting to destabilise even further an already unstable Europe.

Though in earlier times the *Abwehr* and SS had had little in common apart from a mutual distrust and dislike, the former military intelligence officer was only too glad to have Barbie working alongside him. Merck's contacts were good, but they were not as good, or as plentiful, as he had led his British masters to believe. Barbie's contacts, on the other hand, were to be found all over Germany and Austria – hundreds of former SS members of the SD and Gestapo. With their help, valuable information about the work of Communist subversives flowed into the files of the British Secret Service.

Barbie was, however, faced with a monumental problem. Though the Secret Service were content to use him – and, through Merck, to pay him – they could not protect him. He was still a wanted war criminal who was being hunted assiduously by the British, Americans and French. No amount of involvement in the crusade against Communism was going to save him from them or the hangman's rope.

It became a matter of urgency to have the telltale blood-group tattoo under his arm removed, the unmistakable mark of an SS man. In November 1946 Barbie and two companions travelled to the house of a 'safe' doctor in Hamburg. They stayed for two days while their tattoos were removed, then caught a tram to the station to board the Hanover train. All the way to the station Barbie was restless. His instinct told him they were being followed. Several times he caught a glimpse of a green sedan behind the tram; it was still there when they arrived at Hamburg station. Nervously the trio edged on to the platform to wait for their train.

Suddenly Barbie felt himself grabbed from behind. His arms were pinioned and he was flung face down on the platform, spreadeagled beneath a burly British soldier. He was taken into an office and, he claimed, beaten up before he and his two companions, stripped of their papers and possessions, were thrown into the cellars of an old house that had been converted into a makeshift prison.

They remained there for three days, yet were never interrogated. On the third day a British officer brought them some food and apologised for the fact that they had not been allowed to take any exercise. The reason, he explained, was that he was on duty alone and therefore could not guard them if they were allowed out of their cells. It was a curious admission to make. Half an hour later the SS men were even more bemused when they heard the sound of a flute being played upstairs. A solitary, flute-playing guard? It seemed too much to hope for. Barbie began casting round for some means of forcing the lock to his cell. In one corner there was a stout piece of iron. Almost too good to be true. . . .

Within minutes the trio were free, cautiously climbing the cellar staircase with Barbie in the lead. In a ground-floor room, sitting with his back to them, the officer was wholly engrossed in his playing. Barbie seized a shovel that was propped against the wall and holding it high, began to creep forward, intent on braining the man. One of his companions plucked his sleeve, frowned and shook his head. Barbie hesitated, then nodded his understanding – the murder of a British officer would achieve nothing other than guaranteeing an even more violent hue and cry once their escape was discovered. Silently they tiptoed past his back to the door. With the clear, mellow tones of the flute echoing in their ears, they let themselves out, clambered over a wall and set off down the road at a brisk pace.

They had escaped with almost sinister ease. The officer's admission that he was alone, the providential piece of iron

that provided a ready-made jemmy, the lack of interrogation
... were these pointers to the possibility that the British
Secret Service had ordered that the men be allowed to
escape? That is an enigma to which we will never find an
answer.

Without papers the three men were vulnerable, liable to
instant re-arrest. They dared not take the train to Hanover,
even if they could somehow find money to purchase fresh
tickets, for all travellers' documents were carefully checked
at the start and end of journeys. They decided that the safest
course was to walk to Marburg, a distance of some 200
miles, trekking across open country to avoid roadblocks and
patrols.

Soon after they left Hamburg they were arrested again,
this time by an armed German watchman. Once more
Barbie's astonishing luck held out – the man turned out to
be a former member of the SS. With a wink at their lack of
papers he let them go.

Several days later they arrived back in Marburg, relieved,
if footsore, to be back on familiar territory. Within three
days all three acquired fresh identity papers. They were the
finest forgeries that money could buy and Barbie was sufficiently emboldened to use them to travel to Kassel to spend
Christmas with his family and to see his new son.

At around the same time he swapped allegiances and
began working for the Americans, once again trailing in the
wake of Kurt Merck who, having largely served his purpose
as far as the British were concerned, had now been dropped
by them. Merck promptly offered his services to the
Americans who snapped him up. Barbie's collection of
agents, his knowledge of anti-Communist operations and his
network of former SS officers were all part of the deal.

As the British and Americans were working on contingency plans for a possible guerrilla uprising in Albania and
Rumania to free them of Communist domination, there was
ample scope for the ex-SS officer's talents as a recruiter.
Even so, his earliest dealings with the Americans brought

him within a whisker of disaster.

The Balkans operation was being masterminded by the US Department of Army Detachment (DAD), which had offices in the I.G. Farben building in Frankfurt where they liaised with British agents working under the cover of the British High Commission. Late in 1946 John Willms, an American agent with the Counter Intelligence Corps was ordered to report to the Farben building where three American civilians were waiting for him. They offered neither their names nor any information about which of the intelligence agencies employed them. With them was a German whom Willms instantly recognised as Barbie.

His job, Willms was told, was to take Barbie to a French intelligence team in an office across the road, to sit with him throughout the interrogation and then return him safely to the Farben building. The hatred on the faces of the Frenchmen when they came face to face with the Butcher of Lyon was unmistakeable. Willms was alarmed to hear the team leader trying to persuade him to leave the room for a few minutes. In his absence, the man said, they would shoot Barbie and then claim that he had been gunned down while attempting to escape. The American refused and sat steadfastly with his charge throughout the interrogation, returning Barbie safely to the DAD office that evening.

Yet at the same time that DAD was covering Barbie, Counter Intelligence Corps officers placed his name on the automatic arrest list as a category-one war criminal!

A year later Barbie was still working for the Americans.

In December 1947 Major Earl Browning, operations officer at CIC headquarters in Frankfurt, initiated a central register of all agents and informants used by the Americans. When the list was complete Browning was astounded to see that it contained the name of Barbie . . . the same name that figured so prominently on his organisation's instant arrest list. An urgent message was sent to the headquarters of CIC's Region IV in Munich: 'Drop Barbie from operations and arrest him.'

Back came the reply, Barbie had 'escaped' before the

order could be carried out. Suspecting something rotten in the state of Bavaria, a special investigation team was despatched to Munich but it discovered little of note. In fact, Barbie was under the protection of the shadowy and obscure organisation, DAD, whose operations were so secret that even the name DAD remained classified until February 1983. In 1948 many DAD agents found themselves with a new acronym – CIA, the Central Intelligence Agency.

Shielded from his hunters in a DAD 'safe house' in the Bavarian town of Memmingen, Barbie was slowly piecing together vital information about the Soviet explorations for uranium ore in Czechoslovakia, the first disturbing hints that Russia was about to enter the nuclear power arena. As it became more and more obvious that a dramatic shift in the balance of power was imminent, the intelligence reports compiled by Barbie were of increasing value to the Americans. They, and his ever-growing dossiers on Communists agitators, were his insurance against arrest. Repeated requests by the French for Barbie to be handed over – they had sentenced him to death *in absentia* on 16 May 1947 – were met with bland denials of his whereabouts by the Americans. The man who 'ran' Barbie, Ebhard Dabringhaus, was ordered to lie to the French on two occasions when they came looking for his charge.

Dabringhaus, a former military intelligence officer, had left the army, but had been offered a job as a civilian agent with the CIC. In the spring of 1948 he found himself in the novel position of 'minding' the man whom his employers were supposedly hunting. It was a crazy situation, Barbie's name appearing simultaneously on the wanted list and on the payroll!

Acting on orders from his CIC superiors, Dabringhaus moved Barbie from Memmingen to a new safe house in Stadtbergen, near the Bavarian town of Augsburg. There, at 10 Mozartstrasse, he lived with Regina, Ute and Klaus-Georg under a variety of aliases: Spehr, Behrends, Mertens, Holzer and, finally Altmann. Each set of identity documents, however, always bore the same Christian name – Klaus – and the same date and place of birth, Bad Godesberg, 25 October, 1913.

The CIC agent, who today is a university professor in America, became increasingly concerned as he began to realise just what sort of man he was protecting – not some minor functionary of the Nazi machine but a major war criminal. When Barbie's partner, the ex-*Abwehr* officer Kurt Merck, warned him that 'if the French ever find out about the mass graves in Lyon, not even Eisenhower will be able to save Barbie', he immediately informed his superiors of his charge's true background, but was reassured that the German would be handed over to the French just as soon as his usefulness was at an end.

That Barbie's usefulness was far from over soon became apparent. Unlike most informants, who received German marks or packets of cigarettes, he was paid in cash in American dollars. The money arrived in a sealed envelope but one day Dabringhaus peeked inside and was astounded to see that the money totalled $1,700, a considerable sum, even if Barbie was dividing it with Merck. Soon afterwards, Dabringhaus, handed Barbie over to another 'minder' and rejoined the army as a major in the Military Intelligence Service.

'Herr Altmann's' new mentor was Sergeant Herbert Bechtold, a 28-year-old Rhinelander who had emigrated to the USA in the thirties. Bechtold lived in the same house as the Barbie family and at night the two men would often go carousing. By day they sought to attract informants from the Bavarian Communist Party by a combination of bribery and blackmail, techniques Barbie had long ago learned in Lyon.

But if his experiences in the French city stood him in good stead in his present circumstances, the reputation he had gained there kept coming back to haunt him. The French continued to press for information about his whereabouts and, several times, sought his extradition through the US

State Department. Each request was met with lies, which infuriated the French because they knew perfectly well that Barbie was being protected by the Americans.

Sergeant Bechtold's superior was Major Eugene Kolb. In a BBC television interview in July 1983 he explained why the State Department stonewalled the French for so long.

> Our principal reason for keeping him away from the French was that we were highly certain, with good reason, that French intelligence agencies, as well as the French *Sureté*, had been thoroughly penetrated by elements of the Communist Party and by the KGB. We were reasonably certain that their first order of business with Barbie, had they been able to get him, would be to interrogate him about our operations and the sources he had recruited for us. Everything else would have taken second place. So we had to protect Barbie.
>
> At one time we heard in Augsburg that a French team, or a team of officers presumed to be from French intelligence, was looking for Barbie to interrogate him. When that happened, we told Barbie to stay home for a while until the team had departed.

On 25 November, 1954 a French court once again passed sentence of death on Klaus Barbie. But he was not there to hear it; by then he had long gone, like so many Nazis before him, to South America, smuggled there by American secret servicemen at the US taxpayers' expense along the aptly named 'Rat Line'.

Between Russia and Poland lies a marshy area of land that is known variously as White Russia, Belarus and Byelorussia; the primitive land that for centuries has been the traditional battleground of eastern Europe. It is a superstitious place, full of hatreds and feuds, and until Hitler's Holocaust it was also the home of the densest concentration of Jews in the world.

When, in June 1941, Germany broke its 'Pact of Steel' with Russia and invaded its erstwhile ally, the advancing *Wehrmacht* soldiers were hailed as liberators by the White Russians who saw Hitler as a saviour who would free them from Soviet domination. A Nazi puppet government was installed in the capital, Minsk, and many White Russians volunteered for service with the SS. The unit they formed was named the Belarus Brigade.

When Heydrich's battalion-strength *Einsatzgruppen*, the task force of political terror, arrived in the Occupied territories to begin their grisly work of mass extermination, nowhere were they more welcomed than in Belarus. Their main targets, as always, were Jews and Communists. The White Russians, who loathed both with equal ferocity, were only too willing to collaborate.

As enthusiastic auxiliaries of the *Einsatzgruppen* they persecuted their fellow-countrymen with a fanatical cruelty that appalled even hardened German SS men. They organised the mass slaughter of Jews, forcing them to the edge of trench-like graves before machine-gunning them into the depths. The younger women were kept back and raped repeatedly before they, too, were despatched by a hail of gunfire. Young children and babies were often not shot, presumably to save ammunition. They would either be tossed, screaming, into the grave on top of the pile of bodies that often included their parents before being suffocated as earth was bulldozed on top of them, or they would be seized by Byelorussian policemen who would swing them by the heels to smash their skulls against rocks or tree trunks. A favourite trick of the Belarus Brigade was to drop children down a well and, as they floundered to stay afloat, toss grenades on top of them.

Many of those White Russians emigrated to the USA at the end of the war. Some are still alive today, living in a New Jersey town called South River. By what means could such inhuman slaughterers have been granted American citizenship? This was the question to which John Loftus was

ordered to find the answer in May 1979, when he accepted
the post of federal prosecutor in the Office of Special Investigations of the Criminal Division of the US Justice Department – the unit investigating Nazi war crimes.

For two and a half years he coordinated a highly secret
inquiry called the 'Belarus Project', during which time he
uncovered proof that many members of that infamous SS
brigade and other Nazi collaborators had been granted US
citizenship as a reward for their cooperation with the
American secret service during its anti-Communist operations in Europe after the war. His findings shook America
and the repercussions are still reverberating round the White
House, Senate and Congress. The story of US complicity in
rescuing White Russian war criminals from justice is the
subject of Loftus's compelling book, *The Belarus Secret*,
published in 1982.

Soon after the book came out, the *New York Times*
printed a story in which Ebhard Dabringhaus admitted that,
as a CIC agent, he had 'minded' Barbie in Bavaria. John
Loftus promptly directed his talents as an investigator to
discovering the truth of this blurred and shadowy period of
le Boucher's life. It was a story that was to grow curiouser
and curiouser.

Loftus interviewed Dabringhaus, who confirmed that
when he had been recruited to undercover work he believed
himself to be employed by the Counter Intelligence Corps.
When questioned about the forms and accounting proced-
ures of the CIC, however, he seemed genuinely baffled and
could not answer. Moreover, the information with which
Barbie provided him was offensive intelligence against
foreign countries. The CIC's business was exclusively that of
counter intelligence.

Perplexed by these contradictions, Loftus asked Dabringhaus the name of his unit. The former agent had difficulty
remembering it but finally came up with the 970th CIC and
added that he thought it had been renumbered the 7247th
CIC towards the end of 1948. Loftus sat up when he heard

the second number. His earlier investigations had uncovered the fact that in the autumn of 1948 several non-military intelligence units operating under army cover had converted to four-figure numbers with the prefix 7. The real CIC had discovered the subterfuge and had protested all the way to the Pentagon. Could it be that Dabringhaus, genuinely believing himself to be a civilian employee of the CIC, had been used by some other intelligence agency so that, if Barbie was ever caught, the CIC would get the blame?

Loftus contacted retured CIC and CIA officers who had helped with his 'Belarus Project'. Their enquiries revealed that none of Barbie's 'CIC' reports had ever reached CIC headquarters. So who *was* he working for? There *had* been a secret cover unit operating in that part of Bavaria but it was parented neither by the CIC nor the newly emerging CIA.

There could be only one answer — the mysterious unit must have operated under the umbrella of the only remaining intelligence-gathering agency: the State Department. But how was he to prove such a political hot potato?

Help came, unexpectedly, from the French. The French government had just released its half of the 1949–50 correspondence with the State Department concerning Barbie. In July 1949 and March 1950 they had requested Barbie's extradition but the reply had been that no one knew his whereabouts. Finally, in May 1950, the French wrote saying that they knew Barbie was in the custody of US intelligence. Their request for him to be turned over to them was turned down when they refused to give an undertaking to return him safely to the Americans. The name of the State Department official who had handled the case was, said the French, a 'Mr Bovie'.

Records showed no such name. However, a Robert A. Bowie had been General Counsel to the High Commissioner of Germany at the right time and had gone on to become Deputy Director of Intelligence for the CIA when Jimmy Carter was serving his term as president. Had he been a CIA agent back in 1949–50? Loftus sought his answer from several independent sources. All confirmed that Bowie's connection with the CIA had not begun until three decades later; at the time when he was corresponding with the French over Barbie he was a legitimate attorney for the High Commissioner.

Loftus tried to obtain Bowie's policy and planning files, supposedly declassified under the thirty-year rule and passed to the National Archives Classified Files section. Yet the State Department had at first refused to hand them over. Subsequently they offered to release them only if the archivists agreed to keep them under lock and key. No such assurance could be given and so the files remained in State Department hands, though officials promised to hire two consultants to declassify them.

Long after the deadline by which the law demanded release of the files, the 'consultants' – former intelligence officers – were still engaged in their lengthy 'review' of the documents. Whatever was in Bowie's policy and planning files was still so sensitive that it warranted a shameless and illegal cover-up. Even when Loftus eventually traced some of the files he found they had been 'laundered' by experts, stripped of all but the most innocuous documentation. The last Barbie file, concerning French requests for his extradition, was missing completely.

One acronym kept reappearing during Loftus's investigations, that of OPC (Office of Policy Coordination), a branch of the State Department dedicated to the overthrow of Communist regimes through propaganda, sabotage, economic warfare and subversion – in fact it was what has since come to be known as a 'dirty tricks' brigade'. The demand for OPC operations emanated from the highest political and military levels. The only limiting factor they laid down was that of 'deniability' – the proviso that, if any operation went foul or was blown, the Secretary of State should be left with enough face-saving plausibility to disavow all knowledge of its existence.

Did Barbie work for OPC?

Loftus continued to press former members, but his questions went unanswered. Several said that Barbie's escape had been engineered by the 'highest zonal authorities' in Germany, but then lapsed into silence once more. Finally he received some sort of answer, but from a non-American source. 'It wasn't the State Department,' revealed the contact. 'Barbie was first and foremost an agent of the British Secret Service.' Certainly the British had not proved averse to using Nazis to counter the spread of Communism in Europe. Apart from employing Barbie, they had released SS-*Brigadeführer* (Brigadier) Walter Schellenberg, former head of the *Ausland*-SD (Foreign Intelligence branch of the SS), and flown him from London to Germany to reconstitute his wartime anti-Soviet operations.

These were not exactly fresh secrets, Loftus realised, so why did enquiry after enquiry come up against a blank wall? The answer – or part of it, at any rate – lies in a curious agreement between the British and American intelligence communities. It has long been demanded by the British Secret Service, as a condition for sharing information with any American intelligence agency, that such information should be divulged to no one without express British permission. So stringent is this directive that American secret servicemen cannot disclose even to their own Justice Department the content of any file of British origin.

Not surprisingly this arrangement finds little favour with the Americans, especially in view of the numerous spy scandals which have rocked Whitehall since the war. In their eyes the British Intelligence services which, unlike their own, are subject to precious little parliamentary control, are as leaky as a colander. America has a Freedom of Information Act; Britain does not. All too often, the Americans believe, the Official Secrets Act is used to prevent political embarrassment rather than to preserve state secrets. Why should they safeguard British secrets which, all too often, the British cannot safeguard themselves? Nonetheless they continue to uphold the agreement because, despite their reservations about British security, they recognise that British intelligence is of high quality and is extremely useful to them.

The conclusion is, then, that the Barbie files have been sanitised, some perhaps permanently shredded, because they contain information that the British still consider to be a threat to their national security. Or, more cynically, that the facts of the case might, even after all these years, prove an embarrassment to Whitehall. Which of these is true and what those facts are few people know. Nothing I have discovered during the course of my research has given me the faintest clue.

One day – perhaps – the enigma may be answered, if and when the relevant Secret Service files are passed to the Public Records Office in London. Only then will the final chapter of the extraordinary career of the Butcher of Lyon be written. And by then it will be a posthumous chapter.

On Sunday 11 March 1951, as the church bells tolled in the Italian seaport of Genoa, the liner *Corrientes* cast off her moorings and slipped away from the quayside into the Mediterranean. It was a noisy, tearful departure, for Italians are emotional and demonstrative folk; the waving, sobbing and crying of farewells went on until long after those on board, bound for Buenos Aires, were out of earshot.

Klaus Altmann and his wife Regina had no one to wave them off save a taciturn American secret service agent who watched the ship leave with no emotion other than relief. The couple stood quietly at the rail, aloof from and unmoved by the rowdy display of Italian sentimentality. Only their children, 9-year-old Ute and Klaus-Georg, aged $4\frac{1}{2}$, were excited by the bustle of departure.

The sailing of the *Corrientes* was the culmination of a month's hard work by those American officials, among them men of the infant CIA, whose job it was to run the 'Rat Line', an operation as cynical as its name. Formed in Austria in 1945, its *raison d'être* was originally honourable enough –

that of helping foreign agents who had been useful to the
United States during the war to escape from Russian-held
territory, men and women whose links with the West could
make them vulnerable to KGB persecution. In the postwar
years, however, such honourable intentions often went out
of the window and the 'Rat Line' was used increasingly to
provide a bolt-hole for more dubious characters than its
intended clients.

None was more unsavoury than 'Herr Klaus Altmann
from Kronstad, occupation mechanic'. That was the descrip-
tion printed on Barbie's phoney travel document, No.
01211454, issued by the American High Commission in
Munich on 21 February, 1951. The documentation had been
acquired under false pretences by the US Counter Intelligence Corps – their reward to a loyal and hard-working
servant.

For three years they had protected him and paid him
handsomely for his help in the clandestine and undeclared
war against Communism, despite many French demands
that he be handed over to stand trial for his crimes against
humanity. They had seen fit to ignore these demands for
three reasons. The first was genuine enough: Barbie had
matured into a first-class undercover man and was of enormous use to them. The second smacks more of self-justifica-
tion: they saw Barbie's operations against the Resistance as
acts of war rather than as crimes. Of his operations against
the Jews they said nothing. . . . The third and most important reason was that they distrusted the French, believing
them to be seeking Barbie's extradition in order to exact
revenge rather than justice. Furthermore, with many former
Resistance men now in high places, they suspected that
France was riddled with Communists.

Major Eugene Kolb, Barbie's American boss in Bavaria,
once said: 'If the French had got Barbie, I have no doubt
that he would have been in Moscow within a few days.' Yet
all the time French demands for Barbie's head were increasing, especially since a US intelligence officer, appalled to

discover that his colleagues were employing 'the Butcher', had leaked news of his whereabouts to his French opposite number.

The time had come to offload Barbie.

Early in February, Leo Hecht, a CIC agent in Augsburg, arranged a farewell meeting between Frau Anna Barbie and her son Klaus. It was a tearful parting, for Frau Barbie was 65 and must have suspected that she would never see her son again. The family was loaded on to an American Army lorry in Stadtbergen and driven to Salzburg in Austria. Though 'Herr and Frau Altmann's' travel documents named their eventual destination as Trieste, they boarded a train for Genoa.

There the party was met by 'the good father', a Croatian priest, Dr Krunoslav Draganovic, who was a valuable US intelligence contact because of his connections with various organisations which handled refugee quotas to South American countries. The priest was holding a photograph of Barbie to identify him when he and his family arrived at Genoa station. He then took them and their CIA 'minder' to a small hotel whose other guests also turned out to be Nazi fugitives making their way down the final stages of the 'Rat Line'.

During the several days that the Barbies spent there, Draganovic settled the final details of their passage to Argentina, for whose government Barbie held a letter of introduction. Notwithstanding the letter, the priest used the time remaining before the sailing of the *Corrientes* to urge Barbie to reconsider his decision and to settle, instead, in Bolivia. There was, he assured the German, a far better future there for him than in Agentina.

As events turned out, the 'good father' was not wrong.

Chapter 9

THE HUNTERS

Helen's daughter was born in a middle-class suburb of Berlin on Monday, 13 February, 1939, eight weeks before Klaus Barbie and Regina Willms announced their engagement. She was christened Beate-Auguste. When she was less than a month old Germany marched into Czechoslovakia and her father, Kurt Kunzel, left his clerk's job in an insurance office and reported for duty with his old infantry regiment.

The Kunzel home was not far from Berlin's Register Office where Barbie married on 25, April 1940. On this day the two of them – SS officer and 14-month-old girl – were in close proximity for a brief time in the city where men would soon begin to plan the 'Final Solution'. Three decades later that systematically planned programme of genocide was to entwine their destines inextricably.

By then Beate had married, was a Parisian housewife and a mother; a strikingly handsome woman with tawny hair and piercing hazel eyes. She was an improbable Nemesis, this lapsed German Protestant who could count Nazi officials among members of her family, yet who became one of the few to prick the conscience of her nation. It was her crusade which helped lodge Barbie behind the bars of Montluc Prison.

On 7 March 1960, three weeks after her 21st birthday, Beate Kunzel disembarked from a train at Paris's Gare du Nord Station to begin work as an au pair and to learn the French language. On being told of her plans her father had exploded. The French capital was, he fumed, the whorehouse of Europe and he confidently predicted that it would

only be a matter of time before his headstrong daughter
ended up hawking herself on the streets around place
Pigalle. He positively forbade her to go. Beate, having made
up her mind, went anyway, and Herr Kunzel learned a
lesson about his daughter's wilful stubborness which others
have discovered to their cost, in the ensuing years.

Two months after her arrival in Paris she met and fell in
love with Serge Klarsfeld, a French Jew of Rumanian
extraction and a student at the School of Political Science.
From him and his family she learned at first hand something
of what her countrymen had inflicted on the Jewish race.
They were stories she had heard neither at home nor at
school. She listened to them with mounting shame.

Serge's mother, Raissa, recounted how her husband,
Arno, a former Foreign Legion soldier who was a member of
the Resistance, had sacrificed his life to save her own and
those of their children. They had lived in Nice and, like
many Jewish families, had built into their home a secret
hiding place, a bolthole in which to secrete themselves on the
day when, inevitably, the Gestapo would come looking for
them.

For the Klarsfeld family that time arrived on the evening
of 30 September 1943, when German policemen involved in
one of the periodic round-ups of Jews came bursting into
their apartment block. Arno, Raissa and their children,
Serge and Tanya, scrambled into the false-walled cubbyhole
they had built into a closet and waited in silence for the
Germans to search the apartment and leave.

They heard the 11-year-old daughter of the couple in the
next apartment open the door and ask the Gestapo men for
identification. In those days it was not unusual for thieves to
take advantage of Jewish fears and pretend to be policemen
in order to rob them of money and jewellery. Her only
answer was a vicious blow across the face with a pistol barrel
which broke her nose. The child's screams as she was beaten
up, her parents' cries of anguish and the shouts of the
Gestapo men were too much for Arno Klarsfeld.

'I'm leaving to save you,' he whispered to Raissa. 'I can stand a concentration camp. I'm strong, but you couldn't take it; neither could the children.' He crawled out and adjusted the false wall behind him. He was waiting for the Germans when they came through the front door. Somehow he convinced them that the family was away in the country while the flat was being disinfected and was curtly ordered to get his clothes together. He pretended to rummage in the closet and slipped his hand through to grip that of his wife. 'Give me the front-door key,' he murmured, kissing her hand. 'And God help you.'

Arno Klarsfeld was 38. He was transported to Auschwitz where he was murdered.

Stories like this and others she heard from Serge's family and friends gradually hardened in Beate a resolve to atone somehow for the crimes which her father's generation had committed in the name of Nazism. The resolve became what might be called Beate's creed:

Until my arrival in France I remained virtually unaware of the Nazi crimes. Nobody at school or in my family had ever unveiled them. When I learned what had really happened between 1933 and 1945 I decided that, in order not to be ashamed of my people and to atone for the crimes perpetrated in its name, it was not sufficient to tell the victims that I sincerely sympathised with their suffering. It was not enough to go to Israel and plant a tree. Instead, I decided to act according to the moral guidelines in which I have always believed.

As a German and not a Jew I think that the great tragedy of the Hitlerian experience cannot be accepted by the Germans as an historic accident, after which we can draw the line of oblivion and non-responsibility. Today Germany is divided into two states, each belonging to one of the two ideological blocs that share the world. I believe in the moral unity of the German people and that, whatever his ideology, each German has specific responsibilities stemming from the death of millions which the Germans brought about forty years ago.

It is not collective guilt, the legacy of the young generations, but rather a collective historic and moral responsibility. It is a terrible challenge to be a German today, for we are not only the sons and daughters of a humanist Germany, that of Goethe, Schiller and Beethoven; we are also the sons and daughters of a monstrous Germany, that of Hitler, Himmler and Eichmann. Each of us inherits not only the good achieved by our people but also the bad; and for us, West or East Germans, this legacy demands a permanent moral involvement in the struggle against the survival of Nazism and against anti-Semitism.

Only when we have achieved our moral rehabilitation will we recover our place among the other peoples of the world. I am what might be called a reunified German and I try to assume these specific responsibilities as a daughter of the German people as a whole.

The victims of the Nazis have the right to expect that new German generations:

1.   Refuse to have the management of German politics entrusted to former Nazis.

2.   Reject the rehabilitation of Nazi criminals, who might be considered the worst in history.

3.   Fight actively against anti-Semitism, help the Jewish people wherever they are persecuted, and remain on the side of the State of Israel in spite of the economic and political interests that the Arab world represents for Germany.

With this unequivocal declaration Beate nailed her colours to the mast. The events to which this commitment were to lead were extraordinary and far-reaching. If contained in a work of fiction, they would be rejected as too fanciful. No novelist would dare invent a middle-class housewife who, between running a home and raising a young family, contrived to travel the world over to track down war criminals, risking prison and even death in the process.

On 7 November 1963 Serge and Beate were married in the town hall of Paris's XVIth *arrondissement* and the new bride began work as a bilingual secretary with the Franco–German Alliance for Youth (OFA) which had recently been established by President de Gaulle and Chancellor Adenauer as a means of building bridges between the two nations. There was a break from work when she gave birth to Arno, named after Serge's father, but in October 1966 she returned to her desk at OFA. Ten months later she was fired – accused of breaking the 'loyalty requirements' of the organisation as a result of a Press article she had written entitled 'Germany's Troubled Sleep'.

In it she had highlighted the National Socialist past of Kurt-Georg Kiesinger, Prime Minister of Württemberg-Baden, who had just announced his intention of seeking election to the Chancellorship of the Federal Republic. Delving into the archives she had reconstructed the politician's career, right from his joining the Nazi Party three months after Hitler took power in 1933 through to the end of the war when he was a senior official concerned with the broadcasting of Nazi propaganda, much of it virulently anti-Semitic.

The Klarsfelds' revelations caused something of a stir but did not affect the outcome of the election. On 12 December 1966 Kiesinger became Chancellor of West Germany.

'I was absolutely horrified,' Mme Klarsfeld told me when we met in her husband's office in Paris in 1983. She went on:

It was not hatred of Kiesinger, nor a morbid fascination with the past that motivated me. It was the awful realisation that, once again, Germany had a National Socialist as Chancellor.

That realisation was the turning point of Serge's and my life. From that moment we decided to fight with every means at our disposal against the rehabilitation of former Nazis. We would fight to win; it would be total war.

Serge's career, our family life, and our material security — all would take second place.

Throughout the election campaign Beate had heckled and harried Kiesinger at public meetings all over Germany, helped by young radicals who had greeted his public appearances with shouts of 'Sieg Heil!' and who had distributed thousands of leaflets chronicling his Nazi roots. But rowdiness and pamphleteering had failed; now that Kiesinger was in power something more dramatic was needed if he were to be unseated.

Beate's plan was daring to the point of foolhardiness and it could easily have cost her her life.

On Thursday, 7 November 1968 she smuggled herself into the annual congress of Kiesinger's party, the Christian Democratic Union (CDU) and, passing herself off as a secretary, managed to bluff her way on to the rostrum. Pretending to wave to someone on the other side of the platform, she began crossing behind the front row of dignitaries. When she drew level with the Chancellor's back, she suddenly lunged at him.

The astounded CDU delegates heard a resounding crack as she slapped him hard across the face, her voice raised in shrill accusation. 'Nazi! Nazi! Nazi!' she yelled as security men leaped on her and bundled her off the stage. She was fortunate to be only manhandled; at least one security man had pulled his gun in the belief that she was a would-be assassin. Only fear of hitting the Chancellor, who was sitting in front of her, his hands clasped to his stinging cheek, prevented the man from opening fire.

Exultant with triumph, Beate allowed herself to be borne off to police headquarters where she was closely questioned by two inspectors, given a meal of sausages and potato salad and locked in a cell. That evening she was hauled before a hastily convened court. She was sentenced to a year's imprisonment. Angrily Beate pointed out that, by marriage, she was a French citizen, and insisted that she be tried by a court convened by the French occupation forces in Berlin. The judge promptly amended her sentence to one of twelve months' suspended.

That slap echoed round the world. And it had the desired effect. Beate Klarsfeld's action and Kiesinger's unsavoury past immediately commanded acres of newsprint and much prime time on radio and television throughout the world. For eleven more months Beate kept up the pressure, heckling Kiesinger at his public appearances and maintaining an unremitting pamphlet campaign against him. Month by month the Chancellor's popularity waned. In September 1969 Kiesinger was toppled in a general election. Germany's new Chancellor, long championed by Beate, was the former Mayor of West Berlin, Willy Brandt.

Cock-a-hoop that she, a young housewife, had been able to stir such a hornets' nest, this remarkable woman turned her attention to fresh targets. Though she was often accused of being a Communist, because of her association with radicals, notably 'Red' Rudi Dutschke, she carried her crusade against anti-Semitism to behind the Iron Curtain. Her uncompromising criticism of Soviet treatment of the Jews landed her in trouble in Warsaw where she was arrested and subsequently expelled from Poland. In Prague she was thrown into prison before the Czech authorities drove her to the Austrian border and kicked her out.

In March 1971 she conceived a harebrained scheme beside which the slapping of Chancellor Kiesinger paled into insignificance: it was nothing less than the armed kidnapping of a wanted Nazi war criminal, *Obersturmbannführer* Kurt Lischka, who had been one of Barbie's wartime superiors. The plan was a bold and desperate one, but it plunged into the realms of broad farce before eventually failing and landing her in another police cell.

Dr Lischka, then 61 years old, lived with his wife in Cologne, making no attempt to hide his identity, despite the fact that twenty years earlier a Paris court had sentenced him in his absence to a term of life imprisonment as punishment for crimes committed when he was senior Gestapo officer responsible for all Jewish affairs in Paris. A committed Nazi, he had joined the party around the same time as Barbie. His membership number was 4538185, Barbie's 4538085.

On Lischka's orders the first mass arrests of German Jews began in 1938. He was an enthusiastic and willing participant in the persecutions of the infamous '*Kristallnacht*', the orgy of destruction against Jewish homes and businesses on 9 November of that year. During the war he was responsible for the arrest of thousands of Jews and their eventual deportation to Auschwitz and other camps. He left France in October 1943 and returned to the RSHA in Berlin where he and his colleague, Herbert Hagen, were deputies to Heinrich Müller, head of the Gestapo. After the war Lischka was captured and interned by the Czechs who, in April 1949, informed the French authorities that the prominent Nazi was in their hands. Inexplicably no request for his extradition was ever despatched from Paris and sixteen months later he was freed.

In 1971 the Klarsfelds went looking for him. They traced his address — 554 Bergisch-Gladbacher Strasse — with ease (one call to directory enquiries in Cologne was enough) and began to plan their commando raid, enlisting the aid of three sympathisers to their cause: Marco, a non-Jewish friend of Serge, and two Jews, Eli, a photographer, and a doctor, David. Their plan was to jump their quarry in a street near his house, blackjack him and then drive him by hire car to where their own car was hidden, deep in a forest on the outskirts of Cologne. There they would transfer the unconscious man to their Renault and race to the Belgian border to cross through into France where the ex-SS man would be handed over to the authorities. As an added inducement and a means of frightening off possible curious passers-by, Beate carried a pistol, though it contained no ammunition and the hammer had been sawn off.

Almost from the start everything began to go awry. By telephone Serge had ordered a Mercedes 220 from the Hertz car rental office in Cologne, choosing that particular model for two reasons. It was Germany's most common model and would therefore attract little attention; in addition it had four doors to ease the bundling of a passenger who would be either unconscious or extremely reluctant into the back seat. Delayed *en route*, the conspirators arrived at the Hertz office later than the agreed time, only to find that the car they had reserved had been let to someone else. The only remaining vehicle was wildly unsuitable – a huge, luxury Mercedes 280. Not only did it have an automatic gearbox, but it had only two doors and was furnished with distinctive out-of-town plates.

The gang trooped off to Avis, but there were bombarded with so many demands for various forms of identification that they returned to Hertz and said they would take the two-door Mercedes after all. Serge had not touched a steering wheel in years and was totally unfamiliar with the intricacies of automatic gearboxes. Nonetheless, as the car had been rented in his name, the Hertz staff would expect to see him driving it away. He slid behind the wheel and fired the engine.

Blipping the throttle with a confidence which he did not feel, he fiddled for a moment or two with the unfamiliar gearshift. There was a roar from the powerful engine and with a squeal of tyres the car bounded forward at an impressive turn of speed, pursued by an irate Hertz manageress yelling: '*Einbahnstrasse! Einbahnstrasse!*' ('One-way street!') Sheepishly he turned round and, at a more sedate pace, pointed the big beige vehicle towards Cologne's busy ring road.

The gang drove out to the secluded forest clearing where their own Renault was hidden, there to rehearse like ballet dancers the sequence of movements needed to cosh and capture their victim. David, the doctor, played the part of

Lischka, being lifted by the others from the back seat of the Mercedes and carried to the Renault. He was rolled into the capacious boot and the lid was slammed on top of him. As the gang congratulated themselves on the smooth transfer, despite the difficulties of getting 'Lischka' through the front door of the Mercedes, one of them asked where the Renault keys were so that David could be freed. There was a muffled yelling from inside the boot and the others bent to listen. 'I've got the keys,' said David. 'They're in my pocket.'

Fortunately the Renault had a boot-lock release beneath the dashboard; as David scrambled out Beate tried to imagine the expression on the face of a garage mechanic who, called to a remote forest clearing to release a car boot, opened the lid to find a man inside it, looking up at him.

That night, back at the hotel, the five gathered to discuss final plans and to practise using their two blackjacks. As they swung imaginary blows at an invisible victim, the head of Eli's cosh flew off its handle and hit the wall with a resounding thump, narrowly missing an antique and expensive-looking mirror. Thenceforth they would have to make do with one cosh.

D-Day was Monday, 22 March, 1971, around 7 a.m. When Lischka appeared, however, the tram stop to which he was heading was so thronged with people that the conspirators lost heart and moved so slowly that their quarry caught his tram without any of them getting close to him. To make matters worse, it began raining heavily. Beate's observations and secret filming of Lischka had revealed that the Nazi returned to the same tram stop each day at 1.25 p.m. That day was no exception and when he dismounted the gang were waiting for him, the engine of the Mercedes ticking over in preparation for the getaway.

The hunters closed in. Eli darted forward, snatched off Lischka's hat and began belabouring him about the head with the remaining blackjack. There seemed to be little effect other than loud bellows for help which quickly attracted a sizeable crowd. The big German — he was well over 6 ft tall – finally sank to his knees on the pavement, more scared than hurt, but the kidnappers could not manhandle him to the car because their way was blocked by a ring of onlookers. As they struggled with the 220-lb deadweight, a smallish, agitated man elbowed his way through the crowd brandishing a police badge in their faces. It was time to quit. Scattering hypodermic syringes and capsules of chloroform, the 'Klarsfeld Gang' fled. As a snatch the whole affair had been a complete fiasco and at first there was almost no publicity in the Press. Neither Lischka nor the Cologne police were anxious to make much fuss; it took Beate, who was becoming a fine exponent of the art of news management, to get the ball rolling and prod the city's news editors into pressing the police for information about the mysterious kidnap attempt.

Seven weeks before the abortive attack on Lischka Chancellor Brandt had signed an important new treaty with France which sent a chill through many a middle-aged and respected West German citizen – one which put an end to the immunity enjoyed since 1954 by war criminals who, despite being sentenced *in absentia* by French courts, continued to live unmolested in their homeland. The Klarsfelds, who had long been tireless campaigners for just such a protocol, were delighted when Brandt, himself an anti-Nazi dissident during the years of the Third Reich, penned his signature to the document in Bonn on 2 February.

The treaty still had to be ratified by the Bundestag, however. Its members, some of whom sympathised with the plight of the ageing Nazis the treaty threatened and others who preferred to let sleeping dogs lie, were dragging their feet, reluctant to give the assent necessary to make the proposals law. The Klarsfelds feared that there was a real danger that, without public pressure on the politicians, the Bundestag would continue to procrastinate or water down the terms of the agreement to such an extent that it would become ineffectual.

The Lischka kidnap had been planned for just that

reason; a headline-grabbing exercise designed to jolt the tardy Bundestag into action under the pressure of public opinion. At the same time the couple had two other arrows to their bow – noisy and well-researched campaigns against two of Lischka's colleagues, both senior officers in the Gestapo in Paris who had been closely involved with the rounding-up of French Jews and their subsequent deportation to the death camps. Like their former comrade, Herbert Hagen and Ernst Heinrichson were enjoying the good life as prosperous businessmen in the booming economy of West Germany, untroubled by a legal system whose officials, in the main, wanted only to forget the dark days of Hitler.

When, in 1974, Beate's constant statements, letters and articles confessing to her part in the kidnap bid finally forced the Cologne prosecutor's office to take action against her for assault, she received a four-month jail sentence which once again splashed the whole affair on to the front pages. Skilfully orchestrated by Serge and her supporters the public outrage and uproar was deafening. How was it possible, people demanded, that a young mother could be locked away in a prison cell for assaulting a known mass murderer, while he and others like him, guilty of crimes unsurpassed in history, were able to walk the street freely, immune from prosecution?

So clamorous was the media campaign that Cologne's public prosecutor was finally dragooned into starting proceedings against the unsavoury trio. On 11 February, 1980 the three-and-a-half-month trial came to an end. During cross-examination Herbert Hagen had refused to discuss his wartime intelligence activities without official permission. In exasperation Prosecutor Friedrich Kaul roared at him: 'What should we do? Ask Herr Hitler for his permission?'

Each man was found guilty of complicity to murder by the deportation of 50,000 Jews from France to Auschwitz. Watched by silent spectators, many wearing the yellow Star of David with the words 'Juif de France', the guilty men bowed their heads as Judge Heinz Fassbender passed sentence on them. Hagen, then 66, was jailed for twelve years. Lischka, aged 70, was sentenced to ten years and Heinrichson, 59, to six years. It had taken nine years of unrelenting pressure by the Klarsfelds to secure justice for crimes committed almost forty years earlier.

Afterwards Serge pronounced his own verdict: 'I am satisfied.' But the demon that drives him and his wife was not. By the time of their Cologne triumph they had spent almost nine years stalking a new quarry.

It was Sunday 25 July 1971, the day after the Jewish Sabbath. Beate Klarsfeld, still in the grip of the obsession that had made her lead the attack on Lischka four months earlier, was busy at work in Paris's IVth *arrondissement*. Ensconced in the offices of the CDJC (Centre de Documentation Juive et Contemporaine) – Jewish Contemporary Documentation Centre – she was poring over a pile of old papers, engrossed in matters dating from darker days three decades earlier. The life's work – for that is what it had become – to which she and her husband had dedicated themselves necessitated their learning in minute detail about the complex and confusing structure of terror that had been at the heart of Hitler's Reich, for only then would they be able to judge the importance and responsibilities of the men they had chosen as their targets.

RSHA, SD, SS, Gestapo, *Kripo, Sipo, Abwehr* – the Nazi penchant for diffusing power by creating overlapping areas of responsibility had built a labyrinth that was difficult to map. The German police machine was often confusing to those who worked in it; to the student of history it is often bafflingly incomprehensible. For that reason Beate had set herself the task of drawing up an operational chart of the German secret services in France, working on the sound principle that it is a good thing to know thine enemy. Slowly she was compiling a vast family tree showing the chains of command and areas of responsibility; a form of gruesome genealogy that would leave her knowing more about the

Nazi apparatus than many of those who were actually employed by it.

The CDJC is a remarkable organisation, a vast and ever-growing archive that garners Nazi documentation of, and Jewish witness to, the Holocaust. Its endless files are crammed with chillingly matter-of-fact reports by German bureaucrats, servicemen and police officers which chronicle crimes on a scale so horrendous that dry, pedantic officialese is perhaps the only means of describing them. Leaning across the wad of original Gestapo documents which Beate was poring over, the director of the library, M. Mazor, handed her a sheaf of recently received papers. 'This will probably interest you,' he said. Beate read them with increasing fury.

Dr Wolfgang Rabl, the public prosecutor of Munich, had recently examined the Barbie file which had landed on his desk from Augsburg after the government of Bavaria's decision to funnel all Nazi war-crimes prosecutions through the state capital. Though, by then, Barbie's whereabouts in South America were known, Dr Rabl showed little indication to seek a prosecution. The treaty signed five months earlier by Willy Brandt had not yet been ratified. That meant that German courts could not try Nazis for crimes against the French — an insistence made by the French in 1954 as they feared that German courts would be too lenient. Yet the West German constitution forbade the extradition of German nationals to stand trial in any other country, so even if Barbie were successfully deported from Bolivia he could neither stand trial in Germany, nor be handed over to the French.

The bewildering Catch-22 situation was complicated even further. The French had already tried Barbie and sentenced him to death on two occasions after finding him guilty of all his known crimes in Lyon and its surrounding territory. The only crime with which, it seemed, he could be freshly charged was the rounding-up and deportation of the forty-one Jewish youngsters from the lonely house on the outskirts of Izieu, on the face of it, an open-and-shut case.

Not so to Rabl. 'The mere fact that on 6 April, 1944 the defendant arrested forty-one children, who were obviously not destined for labour camps, and had them shipped to the concentration camp at Drancy, cannot be interpreted to mean that he knew the eventual destination of those children,' he ruled. His recommendations to his chief, Manfred Ludolph, was that the Barbie case should be dropped. Ludolph concurred and the file was shelved.

Beate was aghast as she read. She recalls:

It dawned on me that the ruling served to rehabilitate, through Barbie, all the Nazi criminals who had operated in France throughout the war. If 'the Butcher' was to get away with it, then what hope would there be of taking action against the other 312 Nazis who were still capable of being prosecuted according to German Law?

I immediately realised that the Barbie case was a landmark, and that we would have to fight relentlessly to get the Munich investigation reopened.

The Klarsfelds had their new crusade.

Chapter 10

EXODUS

In the high Andes, straddling the border between Bolivia and Peru, lies Lake Titicaca. Its size, 3,200 square miles, makes it South America's biggest; its altitude, 12,500 feet above sea level, means it is the world's highest large lake. To the east, in the Los Yungas mountain range of Bolivia, some 6,000 feet above sea level, is a dense, tropical mahogany forest in the heart of which, at Caranavi, Ludwig Kapauner, a German who had emigrated to Bolivia before the war, established a logging camp and sawmill.

It was here that Barbie, under the guise of Klaus Altmann found work as the sawmill's manager, his first real job in South America and a lucky find, for his ignorance of forestry and logging was total. 'I knew nothing about wood, diesel engines or sawmills, and couldn't speak Spanish,' he was to recall. Nonetheless he was hired by the estate's general manager, another German, after a cursory interview comprising two questions: 'Why do you want to work?' and 'Where are you from?'

When he was placed on the payroll and set in charge of the eighty local Indians that made up the workforce, he had not yet met his employer. Herr Kapauner was away on a business trip and did not return until several weeks after his new manager had begun work. When the two men were eventually introduced Kapauner was obviously impressed by 'Herr Altmann's' workmanlike approach to management and his kindly, if distant, rapport with the Indians who had responded by working well for him. Barbie chatted politely with his new boss. Kapauner had emigrated from Germany in the thirties. The Butcher of Lyon was working for a Jew.

The irony increased when Kapauner informed him of what he had seen on his drive to Caranavi. During his absence one of the many right-wing groups that abound in South America had defaced some of his trees with crudely daubed swastikas. It was distressing that old prejudices still lived; perhaps Herr Altmann could arrange to have the trees cleaned of the hated Nazi talisman?

Barbie organised an immediate working party.

Herr and Frau Altmann had arrived in Buenos Aires in April 1951 and, after a brief stay, they took the train to the Bolivian capital of La Paz which stands 12,000 feet above sea level. Those early days were an unhappy time for the couple and their two children. Homesickness, altitude sickness and a fast-dwindling bankroll, meant hard times for the young family. They moved into La Paz's cheapest hotel, little more than a flophouse, and while Regina tried to keep her children fed and amused, her once-elegant husband took to tramping the streets in a shabby suit, looking for work.

Despite his unaccustomed poverty Barbie was not unduly pessimistic about the future. Bolivia was a wildly unstable country with a Hispanic taste for revolution and counter-revolution which, in its 125 years of independence, had inflicted on it almost 200 coups. While the country remained, in consequence, in a permanently poverty-stricken muddle, its many German immigrants prospered by dint of hard work and business acumen. Presidents might come and go but the Germans remained as the cement which held together the business community.

Germans had also trained the Bolivian Army, infusing it with Prussian military traditions during the pre-war years — among them, the leader of the SA, Captain Ernst Röhm. More than half the country's economy was in German hands. Surely, Barbie reasoned, with so many potential *Kamaraden* around it would be only a matter of time before an offer of help was forthcoming. He was right. First came a contract to repair some laboratory equipment, though from what past experience he was able to dredge up the necessary expertise it is hard to imagine. Nonetheless the money he received was sufficient to stave off impending penury.

Then came the real break — a tipoff from a German crony about the job at the Caranavi sawmill. Barbie wasted no time. Somehow he acquired an old lorry and, leaving Regina and the children at the scruffy and malodorous hotel, he set off for the mountains. The drive took two days and was somewhat hair-raising as he took the battered vehicle through 15,000 feet high mountain passes before descending towards the forest past the rusty skeletons of lorries which, failing to negotiate the endless bends, had plunged into deep ravines.

For three years, during which he learned much about trees and wood, Caranavi was Barbie's home. During that time news reached him of his second sentence of death ordered by a tribunal in Lyon. It was time, he decided, to take out a little more insurance in the form of Bolivian citizenship, though his plan ran into initial snags when the German embassy refused to issue him a passport in the name of Klaus Altmann because he lacked the necessary documentation. His tenuous claim to Bolivian residence was still founded on the temporary papers that had been obtained for him in Genoa by the 'Good Father', Dr Draganovic.

Though Bolivian law holds that a person must be resident in the country for ten years before he can be eligible for citizenship, Altmann used his growing circle of contacts among influential right-wing politicians to circumvent the rules and on 10 October, 1957 he became a Bolivian citizen. The papers were signed by the then President, Siles Zuazo, who, after a yo-yo-like political career, regained the presidency and, years later, became the man who kicked Barbie out to stand trial in France.

After three years spent 'recovering from the war' at Caranavi, Herr Altmann made a dramatic change of career. Having modestly prospered in the timber industry in 1954 he decided to go into the shipping business, though he was also totally ignorant of matters maritime. In an office in the Calle Ayacucho, La Paz, he set up the Estrella Shipping Company, despite the fact that Bolivia was landlocked. Sailing from ports in other South American countries in chartered vessels, Estrella was involved in carrying Bolivia's considerable exports of quinine.

By 1960 Barbie had made enough money to buy his own sawmill at the town of Cochabamba, south-east of La Paz, and to install his family in a nearby house, a curious circular edifice built of concrete which bore a startling resemblance to a wartime pillbox. Soon he was earning a considerable income from shipping his own chinin, the wood bark from which quinine is derived, and selling it to a pharmaceutical company in Mannheim. War was raging in Vietnam and the drug was in tremendous demand. Later Barbie was to say: 'For the first time, I became a war profiteer.' Like many of his statements it was a lie; he had long since mastered the art of lining his own pocket with the spoils of war.

There is evidence that Estrella often carried more sinister cargoes than malaria prophylactics. In the never-ending turmoil of Latin American politics, there was a constant and hungry market for arms. Barbie had the contacts; his customers had the money. They got their arms; Barbie became even richer and his circle of powerful friends spread even wider. Not least among his clients were groups of right-wing Bolivians who were constantly jockeying for power in an endless round of coup and counter-coup.

In 1965 Altmann consolidated his grip on the maritime world when he was invited by the new President, René Barrientos, who had taken power after yet another insurrection, to purchase a fleet of ships which would become the core of a mercantile marine for the country. The company was named Transmaritima and was funded by public subscriptions of $50,000 and preferential state loans. Profits were to be divided between Altmann and the government, the latter receiving the lion's share of 51 per cent. The German promptly installed his cronies as executives and appointed his son as the company executive in Hamburg.

The imaginative scheme never materialised. Instead Altmann merely chartered ships and used them to ply his gun-running trade, supplying his own government and other South American juntas. He was also on the fringes of Bolivia's illegal but highly lucrative cocaine-smuggling rackets through his close friendship with Arce Gomez, who is currently in an Argentine prison while the United States seeks his extradition on narcotics-smuggling charges.

Altmann's secret arms deals slowly became more ambitious. As a state employee he was issued with a coveted diplomatic passport under the protection of which he was able to fly to Germany, the USA, the Bahamas (to deposit money in a discreet bank account) and even, he claimed, France. In Paris, he claims to have visited the tomb of Jean Moulin. 'It may seem strange, but I placed a bunch of flowers on his tomb,' he told a reporter later. 'We had been enemies, but he had been a very brave man and I had admired his courage.'

His biggest coup was the purchase of thirty Austrian armoured cars, together with other weapons, in the late seventies. The front man for the deal was Alvaro de Castro, a representative of the manufacturers, Steyr-Daimler. He later became the SS man's personal bodyguard and closest friend.

But undoubtedly his most spectacularly bare-faced deal had been after the Middle East war of 1967 when he flew to Belgium to secure a massive supply of small arms which the manufacturers believed were destined for the Bolivian Army. Instead, the former Gestapo chief used Trans-maritima to divert the weapons to a new customer whose usual supplies had dried up in the face of an arms embargo – the State of Israel. This, surely, was the supreme irony. News of this bizarre deal was somehow leaked and a Bolivian journalist, Otero Calderon, managed to acquire some papers relating to the affair. His scoop never materialised. One morning he was shot dead at his office in La Paz and the incriminating documents vanished. A few days later Alfredo Alexander, a Bolivian diplomat who had been involved in the deal, was killed – as was his wife – by a parcel bomb.

The following year, on 5 June 1968, Klaus and Regina Altmann celebrated the wedding of their son, Klaus-Georg, to a French girl, Françoise Craxier-Roux, whom he had met in Europe. Ute, who had gone to school in Austria, had joined the teaching profession and was an English tutor at the grammar school in Kufstein, a resort in the Austrian Kaiser Mountains. There, in 1976, she married the recently divorced head of chemistry and physics at the school, Professor 'Heini' Messner. Today they live in a modest flat in the town's Kaiserbach street.

Though Barbie's murky dealings on the international arms market had made him a wealthy man, the Bolivian people who had contributed to the formation of Transmaritima did not share that wealth – their 'lion's share' turned out to be a share of nothing. By 1970 the company was on the point of collapse, plagued by vast debts that totalled more than eight times the initial capital. In 1971 Barbie was removed from the board and alarmed foreign creditors began issuing writs in a bid to recoup some of their losses from the company's assets. That is when the bubble burst – Transmaritima *had* no assets, thanks to Barbie's policy of chartering rather than buying. And what profits had been made had long ago been milked into his own secret bank account in the Bahamas.

The SS man had been uncomfortable for some time. In 1970 he had quietly slipped over the border into Peru when a left-wing general, Juan José Torres, had briefly come to power in La Paz. In 1971, however, he returned when still another coup placed his friend and patron Hugo Banzer, a right-winger of German stock, in power. Banzer talked the same language as Barbie and, on 22 August, took over the presidential palace, avowing his dedication to the destruction of Communism and the suppression of trade unions. All political parties were banned and a cabinet was formed from the ranks of the military.

The Transmaritima affair was quickly forgotten. 'Don Klaus' was too good a friend of the junta to be faced with any embarrassing questions about such a trifling matter. The Bolivian public, brought up from birth with an almost fatalistic acceptance of governmental corruption, shrugged their shoulders; then they, too, forgot.

In January 1972 Beate Klarsfeld announced to the world that Klaus Altmann was none other than Klaus Barbie, the Butcher of Lyon. Barbie issued a denial but when the French government applied to Bolivia for his extradition, he prudently slipped over the border into Peru once more. This time, however, the Peruvian authorities declared him *persona non grata* and he was escorted back to the border at Lake Titicaca where he was handed over to Bolivian immigration officials.

President Banzer's patronage would now be put to the acid test. Would Barbie continue to enjoy his confidence and support? Or would the President hand him over to the French? Banzer kept faith, and, a year later, Barbie spent seven months in comfortable 'protective custody' in La Paz's San Pedro prison where he was treated as a man of prestige.

In La Paz the Supreme Court continued to dither over the French extradition bid, asking somewhat querulously among themselves whether or not Barbie could be counted as a Bolivian citizen when he had been naturalised under a false name. Finally Banzer himself put an end to it by declaring that the judges were a bunch of incompetents and threatening to sack them if they didn't show a more pragmatic approach to political problems.

His irritation produced quick results. On 5 July, 1973 the judges turned down the French application on three grounds: that no extradition treaty existed between the two countries; that Barbie was a bona-fide Bolivian; and that the Bolivian legal code did not recognise the existence of war crimes.

Barbie was grateful for Banzer's timely intervention and over the next few years demonstrated his gratitude amply. As the regime brutally suppressed all opposition, murdering Communists and trade-unionists, Barbie dovetailed happily into the role of part-time consultant on matters of security, counter-subversion and intelligence. As ever, he shone in the field of winkling out Communists who, for years, had been fomenting strife and revolution in Latin America. In these efforts he once again began to serve the Americans, albeit indirectly.

America's understandable fears about the spread of Communism through South and Central America had led to considerable activity in the continent by the CIA and the US Special Forces (the 'Green Berets'). The latter, a mobile force of crack jungle fighters, had been involved in suppressing the Che Guevara movement and had enlisted the help of the Bolivian intelligence authorities. When Guevara was captured and killed in 1967 other revolutionaries and 'freedom fighters' took his place. A considerable portion of the intelligence about their activities was passed to the Americans by Barbie via the Bolivian Secret Service.

In the summer of 1978 anarchy ruled in Bolivia. Banzer resigned and left the country in some haste to be succeeded by no less than six presidents in the next two years. The self-mutilation of Bolivian politics saw to it that during the short reigns of those six men the country underwent three elections and three coups. The last upheaval had given an election majority to Siles Zuazo, the former President who had signed Barbie's naturalisation papers. However, his politics were too liberal for the military and they refused to let him take office. An interim government was declared and Bolivia once again was plunged into an orgy of street violence, strikes and demonstrations.

Barbie's cocaine-trafficking friend, Colonel Arce Gomez, let it be known to the SS man that the army commander, General Luis Garcia Meza, was starting to plan a coup to restore firm military control to put an end to the anarchy that was crucifying the country. He – Gomez – would be the general's right-hand man. Would 'Don Klaus' consent to give his help to the forthcoming revolution?

Barbie was flattered. At last here was a chance to play a real role in major matters of state. He accepted with alacrity and travelled with Gomez to Bolivia's 'drug capital', Santa Cruz, to train with a group of European mercenaries who called themselves the Fiancés of Death, among them a 31-year-old deserter from the West German Army, Joachim Fiebelkorn, a neo-Nazi with a taste for strutting around in SS uniform.

Fiebelkorn was believed by the Italian authorites to be the man who planted the bomb at Bologna railway station in August 1980 which killed eighty-five people and seriously injured almost 200 more. The atrocity was planned by two other Fiancés, a pair of Italian Fascists, Stefano Delle Chiaie and Pierluigi Pagliai.

This murderous trio and their gang of paramilitaries alternated between training for the revolution and guarding the cocaine interests of Arce Gomez's cousin and partner, Roberto Suaréz. Those interests were considerable. Thanks to the new fad of 'coke sniffing' by America's east coast socialites by 1982 the racket was estimated to be worth an incredible $400,000,000 a year. From those profits would come money to prop up the new Meza regime, in return for which Suaréz would be allowed to go about his racketeering unmolested.

Santa Cruz, some 250 miles south-east of La Paz, quickly became the fiefdom of the German mafia. Each night in the Bavaria Club, a replica of a German *Bierkeller*, decked out in combat kit or old Nazi uniforms, they indulged themselves in wild drinking sprees and sex orgies. Rousing choruses of the 'Horst Wessel Song' and other Nazi marching tunes echoed through the club, often sung to the accompaniment of pistol shots through the ceiling. On occasions Barbie, the grand old man of the Gestapo, was an honoured guest of the Fiancés, though he prudently distanced himself from their cruder excesses.

In July 1980 he passed word to the mercenaries that the coup was imminent. Fiebelkorn and his men were given the job of breaking up student demonstrations, a task which they tackled with great enthusiasm and brutality. His gang laid fire-bombs at the homes of left-wing politicians and exploded car bombs in the streets. On the day of the actual coup, Thursday 17 July 1980, they ran amok through the town, murdering political leaders and rounding up journalists, students and trade-union officials, many of whom were later tortured and killed by Meza's men. For their cooperation in Bolivia's 189th coup, and at Barbie's suggestion, they were employed by the new government and were given an HQ near Santa Cruz airport.

At the end of 1980 Barbie summoned the leaders of the Fiancés of Death to La Paz for a meeting with the President and the new Minister of the Interior, Colonel Gomez, whose involvement with his cousin's drug-running had earned him the nickname 'Minister of Cocaine'. Every shipment of coca leaves, the staple of cocaine, that was illegally exported brought Gomez a handsome commission, but the Americans were now threatening this lucrative sideline. Washington had been alarmed both by the recent seizure of power by the Meza regime, which they refused to recognise, and by the epidemic proportions of the coke-sniffing craze in the USA.

Anxious to re-establish warmer relations with the United States, which he saw as a bulwark against left-wing revolution in Latin America. President Meza had ordered his Interior Minister to make a conciliatory gesture. This was to take the form of an apparent clamp-down on the smuggling rackets to convince the State Department and US drug agencies that La Paz shared their concern. By so doing, Meza hoped to regain American approval – and a restoration of the economic aid programme which had been terminated when he seized office.

The job of Fiebelkorn and his men was to hunt down 'illegal' drug smugglers – in other words those unconnected with Suaréz's set-up. This they did with a ruthlessness that carried with it echoes of the Gestapo operations in Lyon almost forty years before – midnight raids, interrogations carried out under torture, men and women who simply disappeared. *Nacht und Nebel* had come to Santa Cruz. . . .

Part of each haul of cocaine was handed over to the government's official narcotics agency as 'proof' to Washington of Meza's good faith and commitment to smashing the racket, but this was mere window-dressing. The majority remained in the hands of the Fiancés' political master, Gomez. The charade impressed no one, least of all the Americans. After TV documentaries exposed Gomez's involvement in cocaine, he was forced to resign from office in March 1981. Some months later, under American pressure, President Meza himself relinquished power and the country plummeted into chaos again as the military fought to prevent the new President elect, the ubiquitous Siles Zuazo, from returning to the presidential palace from exile in Peru.

Zuazo bided his time in Peru and a week later the presidency changed yet again. This time the incumbent was General Guido Vildoso, a choice which suited Barbie. He had been worried by interviews which Zuazo had given in Peru during which he had stated that, when he returned to power, he would end the protection which the Nazi fugitive had enjoyed for so long. Vildoso, on the other hand, was Barbie's kind of man, a right-winger and a soldier. Any lingering illusions that the new president might honour Zuazo's pledge regarding Barbie were quickly dispelled when, eight days after taking office, he received his first private visitor to the presidential palace.

It was Barbie.

This proof of presidential approval was heartening, but by then Barbie had been devasted by a personal tragedy. Despite his peripatetic lifestyle, the family home had, since 1960, been the house at the sawmill he had established at Cochabamba. There, on Labour Day, Friday, 1 May 1981, he and Regina climbed into their car and drove to open country near the town of Tunari to watch Klaus junior hang-gliding. Both parents had been worried when the 34-year-old – now the father of three children – had taken up the dangerous sport. Frau Barbie had begged him to find a safer pastime but her son had laughed off her fears.

Now, tragically, they were realised. Klaus launched himself, strapped to the frail, dartlike device, from the top of a cliff, dipping briefly until the wings caught the wind. Riding on an updraught, he soared gracefully upwards as the Barbies craned their necks to watch. Without warning a sudden squall caused the hang-glider to buck and sheer. It dropped a wing, stalled and tumbled clumsily to earth, smashing in a welter of splinters only yards from Klaus's horrified parents. By the time they reached him he was dead.

On 6 October 1982, nineteen days before Barbie's 69th birthday, the see-saw politics of Bolivia brought Siles Zuazo back as President and a fragile democracy returned to the country. Despite the fact that Zuazo had said of Barbie: 'We will extradite him. We have no interest in protecting people like him,' – despite the fact that at last the Klarsfelds' campaign had stirred Bonn into formally requesting his extradition, he himself did not appear worried. Over coffee at his favourite haunt in La Paz he told journalists: 'I'm not worried about the German extradition demand. Bolivian law rules here.'

As things turned out, he was correct to be untroubled by the Germans. The nation that should, however, have caused him concern was France, from whose clutches he had managed to duck and weave for so long. But by this time personal matters were once more weighing on his mind. Still distraught from the death of his son, he had become worried about his wife's health. For some weeks she had been complaining of stomach pains and he had brought her from Cochabamba for a series of tests at a La Paz clinic. There, a grave-faced doctor broke the news that Barbie had feared all along. The diagnosis was cancer, inoperable and terminal. Regina died just before Christmas 1982, aged 66, and was buried in the capital's German cemetery beside her son, among the graves of her husband's dead comrades.

Stunned by the double tragedy, he moved to Santa Cruz to live with his daughter-in-law and her three children. He was 69 years old, dispirited and lonely. Ute was thousands of miles away in Austria, and one by one his old cronies, once the young lions of the Third Reich, were dying off. Even the heady days of the latter-day storm-troopers of the Fiancés of Death were behind him. They had fled the country a year before, close on the heels of their disgraced patron, ex-President Meza. He and Arce Gomez had escaped with millions of dollars apiece and taken refuge in Argentina where a hard-line general called Leopoldo Galtieri was already scheming his own political adventures.

While Barbie, suddenly frail and old, mourned the past, his fate was being decided by a series of complex and delicate diplomatic moves involving the United States, Germany, France, and Bolivia. These moves were concerned more with political expediency and face-saving than they were with justice, but the end result was the same. Time was fast running out for the Butcher.

America, anxious to keep Bolivia within its sphere of influence, was willing to give the Zuazo government generous loans. But constant criticism of US involvement in Latin America had made Washington hypersensitive about accusations of propping up corrupt right-wing regimes. The world had to see that Zuazo was making every effort to rid his country of Nazi fugitives. Bolivia, in its turn, wanted the US loans, and therefore wanted rid of Barbie, the most notorious of those fugitives. President Zuazo did not, however, want to be seen to be dancing to any other nation's tune and therefore insisted that he be dispensed with in a totally legal fashion — no easy feat when the Supreme Court had already ruled that Barbie could be neither extradited nor expelled.

France wanted justice, punishment for the death of Jean Moulin and retribution for the atrocities committed in Lyon and Haute-Savoie. Under pressure from its new left-wing

President Mitterrand the country renewed its demands for extradition. Yet there was ambivalence even in the French attitude, for there were many people, some in high places, who had much to fear from revelations which Barbie might make once he was in the dock.

West Germany wanted only to forget Barbie and the Hitler era, yet had to be seen by the international community to be pushing hard for the Gestapo man's return. Earlier war-crimes trials in German courts had attracted much foreign criticism – notably from the French – for their snail-like progress and often derisory sentences. Furthermore, the conservative Chancellor, Helmut Kohl, was due to fight a national election in March 1983. Raking over the cold ashes of the Third Reich might drive the voters towards the liberals and socialists of the SPD.

In January 1983, after a lonely Christmas at Santa Cruz, the focal point of all this diplomatic doublethink returned to La Paz and was summoned by senior civil servants of the new Zuazo regime who demanded repayment of a Transmaritima debt totalling $10,000 and dating from 1968. Truculently Barbie began arguing and was promptly arrested. Next day he was charged with fraud and, for good measure, with contravening Bolivian immigration laws and illegally raising a private army.

President Zuazo's ingenuous hopes that he could rid himself of Barbie by scrupulously legal methods quickly evaporated in the heat of the extraordinary behind-the-scenes diplomatic square-dance that ensued. Desperate to save face and demonstrate Bolivian sovereignty, Zuazo at first insisted that the Gestapo man should leave the country by a non-Bolivian airline, the normal method of extradition, even though the Supreme Court was still deliberating; the same Supreme Court which had already ruled that Barbie could not be extradited.

Lufthansa flew from La Paz to Frankfurt via Lima, a route tailor-made for an easy solution to the problem. The Bolivian Ministry of the Interior called in the German and

French chargés d'affaires, informing them that Barbie would be put aboard this flight. It was no longer proposed, he said, to await the Supreme Court's ruling. In other words, Zuazo's pious insistence that the letter of the law be followed was a fiction; Barbie was to be kicked out by any means possible.

Hour by hour the situation grew more absurd. Though still publicly demanding the extradition, the West Germans let it be known that Barbie would not be allowed into Germany under any circumstances. Nor would he be allowed on the Lufthansa flight. Zuazo, bewildered by all the diplomatic chicanery, begged the two countries to resolve the matter quickly. A French proposal that Barbie be put on the Lufthansa flight and then diverted because of 'bad weather' to the French colony of Guyana was flatly rejected by Bonn. Then President Zuazo reversed his earlier decision. If the prisoner could not be extradited on a German aircraft then he would not be extradited at all. Instead, he would be expelled and that meant he had to fly out on a Bolivian aircraft.

On 2 February matters were further complicated when Carrión Constantino, Barbie's lawyer, paid his client's $10,000 debt, presumably with money raised by La Paz's German community. Furthermore, Constantino was demanding to know why his client had been kept incommunicado for two days and why Bolivia, whose penal system did not recognise the existence of war crimes, was trying to kick Barbie out to face that very charge. His client, he protested, was now Bolivian and not German and, in any case, no extradition treaty existed between Bolivia and West Germany.

Legally, Barbie was on very firm ground. Something akin to panic began to grip Bolivia's 192nd president.

Then Peru dropped a bombshell into the negotiations. Its national airline, Aeroperu, had been ordered not to take Barbie as a passenger and Lufthansa had been warned by Lima that their aircraft would not be allowed to land if he was aboard. So Zuazo seemed stuck with either putting his prisoner across the nearest land border, where he would no doubt vanish, or keeping to his amended plan of flying him somewhere on a Bolivian aircraft. But by then all his country's airline pilots had gone on yet another strike.

In the end it was left to the French to work out a way of breaking the impasse. On the morning of Friday, 4 February Barbie was hustled out of San Pedro prison, his head covered with a blanket, and was driven at high speed to La Paz airport. There he was manacled and informed that he was being expelled for using a false name and forged papers to obtain Bolivian nationality, before being escorted across the tarmac to a four-engined Lockheed C130 Hercules bearing the livery of Lloyds, a privately owned Bolivian airline.

In reality it was a French military aircraft whose blue, white and red roundels and other identifying marks had been painted out. The French crew was silent, speaking to Bolivian officials only in sign language. Barbie, who thought his destination was Germany, seemed relatively untroubled by the proceedings, but complained that he was cold. A policeman handed him his parka.

When in the evening, after a seven-hour flight, the Hercules made its final preparations for landing at Guyana's Cayenne airport north of the mouth of the Amazon, the cabin lights were switched off and Barbie sat in darkness as the big machine clumped on to the runway. The propellers were still turning when the doors were opened. The German peered into the gloom and gasped with disbelief – waiting on the tarmac for his arrival was a knot of soldiers. French soldiers! Among them he could see blue Képis – the men were *gendarmes*.

Stunned at Bolivia's duplicity in delivering him into the hands of his old enemy, he protested that his expulsion was illegal. The police ignored his protestations and, as his feet touched French soil, formally charged him.

Soon afterwards, aboard a military DC-8 – one used by President Mitterrand for official visits – he flew the Atlantic non-stop to the Orange airforce base near Lyon. From there a police van rushed him to Montluc under heavy motorised escort. At a few minutes after 10.30 p.m. on Saturday, 5 February the green iron gates clanged shut behind him.

Less than a week later he was transferred to a special isolation block in the civil prison of St Joseph, a stone's throw across the railway line from his old HQ, the Hôtel Terminus.

Then the legal arguments began.

The charges against Barbie were read to him three weeks after his return to Lyon. There were eight separate counts:

1.   The murder of the commissaire and twenty-two hostages, among them women and children, as a reprisal for an attack on two German policemen in 1943.
2.   The arrest and torture of nineteen people in Lyon in 1943.
3.   The liquidation of the Lyon UGIF committee and the deportation of eighty-six members on 9 February 1943.
4.   The shooting of forty-two people, forty of them Jewish, during 1943 and 1944.
5.   The round-up on 9 August 1944 of railway workers at Ouillins, when two were killed, others wounded and others arrested, final fate unknown.
6.   The deportation to Auschwitz and Ravensbruck of about 650 people, half of them Jews, on the last rail convoy from Lyon on 11 August 1944.
7.   The shooting of seventy Jews at Bron on 17 August 1944 and the shooting of other Jews and two Roman Catholic priests at St Genis-Laval on 20 August 1944.
8.   The deportation of fifty-five Jews, including fifty-two children, from Izieu in 1944.

Some of these figures — notably the number of Jewish children taken from Izieu — are inaccurate, but they were based on French estimates that had been made in the confused days immediately after the liberation of France.

The man who was given the job of investigating the charges was a young and ambitious examining magistrate, Christian Riss, to whom fell the thankless task of dredging up reliable witnesses from forty years previously to testify against the Butcher. The 36-year-old magistrate quickly grew tired of the limelight which the assignment brought him.

He becomes irritable when asked questions about Barbie's special status in St Joseph prison – a whole floor to himself and a twenty-strong team of warders. 'He has exactly the same visits and the same obligations as other prisoners,' he says. This is not true. Unlike other prisoners Barbie can write and receive as many letters as he wants, though all are censored by Riss to expunge them of any mention of events between 1939 and 1945. He has books and newspapers, even a TV set to himself. The only privilege denied him is that of embracing his daughter on her frequent visits; they have to talk through a glass screen.

> We have to be sure that no one gives him anything [Riss explains]. One has to think, of course, of suicide. He is now an old man. He is not well and complains of pains in his legs and back.
> After the death of his wife, we cannot rule out the possibility that he may not want to live.

He becomes angry at suggestions that Barbie's life is in danger from Frenchmen who do not want him to stand trial.

> How could we be so stupid as to let that happen? Can you imagine how it would reflect on us all – the French, France, French justice? It is unthinkable.
> I assure you he is being kept in conditions of maximum security. He has special guards, special arrangements. In fact, Barbie gets such special treatment that we are having trouble from the rest of the prisoners. They are

jealous. Why should Barbie be the star of St Joseph?

His anger mounts even more when questioned about the year's delay in bringing about the trial and the total absence of any sign that proceedings are ever going to get under way.

> It will happen only when I am ready. But I am not the only person involved. We have many witnesses to find, and they are not all in France but are scattered all about the world. I have to find time to go through all the old papers — reports, archives, anything to do with the Germans, collaborators and traitors. It is work for a historian that we are talking about.
>
> You must understand, I am the examining judge for Lyon. Barbie, I am afraid, is not my only concern. He is just one of many dossiers. At the moment, I have a hundred others to prepare and some forty other people in prison awaiting trial.

If the prosecution faces problems, so, too, does the defence. Barbie's first lawyer was Maître Alain de la Servette, president of Lyon's bar association, a quiet, middle-aged man whose shrewd eyes hide behind spectacles with pebble lenses. Courteously, he explained to me why he had taken on such a notorious client:

> Purely in the interests of justice, you understand. My normal practice is commercial law, but as President of the Bar I did not feel it was right that I should delegate the defence to another lawyer. Yet Barbie is just as entitled to justice and a defence as any other accused man. Therefore, I thought it would be the right thing to do to handle the case myself.
>
> When I first went to see him I expected to see an ogre. All I saw was a little old man.

On 5 March Ute Messner travelled from Kufstein to see her

father in his cell. Afterwards she said the reunion had been 'very moving', then told journalists: 'He is still for me my father, a very good father, not a war criminal.'

The following day Barbie collapsed and was rushed to hospital where he was diagnosed as suffering from a strangulated intestine. Was fate going to resolve *l'affaire Barbie*? There were those in France, the USA, and Britain who saw his death as a neat solution to many problems, but the Butcher rallied and made a complete recovery. Ironically, the doctor who pulled him through had been a member of the French Resistance.

Four months after his extradition Barbie changed lawyers. Out went Alain de la Servette to be replaced by Jacques Verges, a left-winger with a long record of championing unpopular causes: members of the Baader-Meinhof gang, Palestine-backed hijackers and Algerian terrorists. The old Nazi's future now lay in the hands of a Marxist.

Chapter 11

RETRIBUTION

Just a line to tell you we Nazis are still around. Even though you are an Aryan, you married a Yid and so, by the rules of our game, you are going to be exterminated.

The Fourth Reich is still at hand. The Crystal Nights and Nuremberg Laws will soon be here again! Twelve million slimy toads like you are going to die this time — and in our new, ultramodern ovens. Half-Jews too! Children of mixed couples are going to be classed as Jews and sent to the crematories.

Best wishes from an Aryan.

A. Hitler

P.S. My house is infested with termites, and my country with Semites. France is a whore of a nation.

The recipient of that letter, one of many similarly couched, sighed deeply. 'Every time I read one,' said Beate Klarsfeld, 'I feel a stab at my heart and I clench my fists. They hurt, but they bolster my determination even more.'

We were talking in her husband's office in rue de la Boétie off the Champs Élysées. She speaks in rapid, idiomatic English, her tone unemotional, as are her feelings towards those she hunts down. She evinces no hatred for them, only for what they have done. She was scornful when I spoke of my efforts to unravel Barbie's complex personality and to understand the man behind the uniform.

To understand what he did to the Jews is sufficient. I don't want to know anything about Barbie other than that which has been necessary to bring him to justice. I don't want to know about the man, the father, the husband – only about the Gestapo officer.

Nor do I want to go to his trial. Why should I go? There is nothing there for me. Now he is the victim; he is in the past. There are others like him to be found in the future.

What we want is for the German government to act, to show the world that the Third Reich is not being allowed to live on. Only by doing this can the government help us once more be proud of being Germans.'

She denies vehemently that her actions are those of the convert, desperately trying to win the approval and acceptance of the Jewish community:

I am married to a Jew, but I am not a Jew myself. Religion means nothing to me. As a German I was accepted immediately by Serge's family, right from the first moment. I am not, as some say, driven by guilt. How can I be guilty of what happened when I was a young child? No, I have no guilt – just a moral and historical responsibility for what the Nazis did to the Jews.

And what of the day when the last of the SS men has died off; when there are no more Gestapo men to hunt down?

Then, perhaps, I shall be able to relax with my grandchildren. But I doubt it; there will always be anti-Semites and neo-Nazis to oppose, and I shall oppose them as long as I have the strength.

At the time Beate was ploughing through the musty old Gestapo and SD dossiers in the CDJC offices in rue Geoffroy d'Asnier, there were in existence 312 files concerning Germans who then – 1971 – were still liable to prosecution in their homeland for war crimes. So the news that Dr Wolfgang Rabl, Munich's public prosecutor, had decided to shelve the Barbie case hit her hard. For the Butcher was one of the most notorious of them all; if he were not being pursued, then what hope was there of proceedings being taken against the rest of them?

With mounting exasperation the Klarsfelds analysed the implications of Rabl's decision. Thanks to the 1954 agreement between France and Germany, war criminals wanted for crimes in France could not be tried in Germany; nor could they be until the tardy Bundestag ratified Willy Brandt's new treaty with the French. Yet, on the other hand, West Germany's constitution expressly forbade the extradition of its nationals to stand trial in any other country. For Barbie it was definitely a case of 'heads I win, tails you lose'.

Though the decision by Rabl, himself a half-Jew, was legally correct, the Klarsfelds hoped it would be only a matter of time before the Brandt protocol drifted through Parliament and put an end to this contradictory legal nonsense. When it did they wanted to be in a position to act quickly.

The files chronicling Barbie's SS career were speedily but methodically sifted for information about his atrocities in Lyon and Haute-Savoie and, within days of the Munich ruling, were receiving widespread publicity in the Press. Gradually the clamour began to mount, criticising Rabl and his chief, Manfred Ludolph, and demanding that the case be resurrected. The campaign gained support, not only from Jewish organisations but also from former members of the French Resistance. Dr Dugougon, in whose villa Jean Moulin had been arrested, said: 'I have prayed to heaven to give me the grace never to sit in judgement, but if I were a judge or a member of a jury, I would sentence Klaus Barbie to death.' He too added his weight to the campaign.

During her researches in the early days of the Barbie affair, Beate had uncovered a document, dated 31 August, 1944, in which Kurt Schendel, a Berlin Jew who had fled to

France before the war, had set out the dealings he had been forced to have with the Gestapo when they appointed him as a UGIF liaison officer. Schendel had been made to attend meetings with several senior Gestapo officers; meetings at which he had courageously argued with them in a bid to save Jewish children from the convoys bound for Auschwitz.

Perhaps day-to-day contact with the Nazis had resulted in Schendel meeting Barbie. On an impulse Beate picked up the Paris telephone directory, found a 'K. Schendel' and dialled the number. There was no reply. She called daily until she got a reply; the subscriber was indeed the man she sought. She arranged a meeting between him, Serge and herself. A few days later, on 8 September, 1971, she received the following affidavit:

> Even in official circles the word 'deportation' was seldom spoken; rather it was 'fit to work', 'evacuation' or 'family reuniting'. In the course of the frequent meetings I was forced to have . . . I soon realised that 'deportation' had dreadful connotations. . . .
>
> Over the course of a year my observations of *Amt IV-B* and the numerous talks I had with its employees, as well as with workers in the other German bureaus, completely convinced me that of them, except perhaps the ones at the very bottom . . . most knew perfectly well what fate awaited the deportees.
>
> I did not know Klaus Barbie personally, but I know that Barbie ordered the arrest of Jews in Lyon and took part in the arrests himself. I have seen reports stating that Barbie persecuted the Jews with intense zeal.
>
> The UGIF branch in Lyon worked independently in the southern zone, but we were constantly in touch with it. Late in 1943 or early 1944, we called a meeting in Paris of its directors, which I attended. There was a great deal of discussion about the summary executions at Fort Montluc of Jews whom Barbie had arrested.
>
> One of the delegates reported that ceaseless attempts

had been made to keep arrested Jews from being shot, but that Barbie had replied: 'Shot or deported – there is no difference.'

Shot or deported – there is no difference. The phrase seemed to leap out from the page. Beate reread it excitedly. Schendel's recollections were mere hearsay and therefore legally inadmissable, but what if the man to whom Barbie had actually spoken the words could be found? His memory of the conversation would be powerful proof that Barbie *had* known the ultimate fate of the Jews, thus challenging Rabl's ruling that there was no reason to suppose he knew the children of Izieu would end up in Auschwitz.

From old files relating to the 1944 UGIF meeting Serge made a list of all the delegates present and set about the laborious chore of tracing and telephoning them. Twenty-eight of them were dead, either victims of the Nazis or of natural causes in the post-war years. In the meantime Beate began trying to contact relatives of the children. Her first find was Mme Benguigi, the tragic mother who had learned of her children's deaths in Auschwitz when she had found her eldest son's clothes among those belonging to a batch of youngsters who had just been gassed. Soon afterwards she traced Itta Halaunbrenner whose husband had been shot by Barbie's men and who had lost two of her three daughters in the ovens of Birkenau and her eldest son in a Polish salt mine.

With their harrowing stories added to her ever bulkier Barbie dossier, she prepared to travel to Munich to protest to Prosecutor Ludolph about his subordinate Rabl's dropping of the case. She contacted Jean Moulin's sister, Laure, and asked her to accompany her. In reply she received a letter which read:

I don't know how to express my admiration for your un-wavering courage in fighting for your country's acknowledgement of its mistakes and of the crimes the Nazis committed.

As I told you over the telephone, I cannot go with you to Munich this month because of my uncertain health, but I want to assure you that I entirely approve of your demonstration. Like you, I strongly protest against the shameful indulgence that the German courts, particularly the Munich court, have shown towards Nazi war criminals and towards that abominable Barbie. . . .

I hold him personally responsible for the death of my brother, Jean Moulin, whom he so maltreated and tortured that he was almost dead by the time Barbie shipped him to Paris on orders from his superiors. Consequently, I am wholly and sincerely with you and with all Frenchmen and Germans who support your plan of action.

If Laure Moulin could not make the journey to Munich, two other women did – Itta Halaunbrenner and Mme Benguigi, who joined Beate and forty former Resistance members led by Dr Dugougon outside Ludolph's chambers in the city's courthouse on Monday, 13 September. He and eleven others formed a delegation which was allowed inside to meet the chief prosecutor, while Beate remained outside.

She was angry on two counts. First, the ex-Resistance men appeared interested only in crimes committed against their wartime colleagues, rather than in Barbie's anti-Jewish atrocities. Second, though they undoubtedly admired her grit, they made it clear that they had little time for her headline-grabbing publicity stunts.

The delegation members were received courteously, but at the end of the meeting received little comfort from Ludolph beyond a vague assurance that he would consider reopening the case if fresh evidence was brought to light by the French. If they were satisfied, Beate was not. When the rest of the party travelled back to Lyon, she and Mme Benguigi stayed on in the Bavarian capital.

The following day was cold and rainy. At 9 a.m. the two

women appeared outside the courthouse in Maxburgstrasse and clambered on to wooden crates they had borrowed from a nearby grocery shop. Each had a large placard. Mme Benguigi's was illustrated by a blown-up picture of her martyred children and read: *I am on hunger strike for as long as the investigation of Klaus Barbie, who murdered my children, remains closed.* Beate's read: *Prosecutor Rabl is rehabilitating war criminals.*

A sympathetic crowd began to gather which grew steadily throughout the day. Tipped off by Beate, the Press and television arrived. The police were called but took no action other than to warn that the sign about Rabl could be construed as libel. Young Germans brought blankets and tit-bits for the two women and spoke comforting words to the elderly Jewess, stroking her hair as they looked sadly at the pictures of her dead family. Words like 'Disgraceful' and 'Shame' were shouted at the courthouse.

By 5 p.m., the crowd around the two wet, cold women had swelled even more as homeward-bound workers stopped to see what was happening. At 6 p.m. Manfred Ludolph bowed to the inevitable and sent a policeman to escort Beate and Mme Benguigi to his chambers.

He greeted them cordially and asked how he could help them.

'By having the Barbie prosecution reopened,' Beate said promptly.

The chief prosecutor began flicking through the dossier which she had sent to his office earlier and began reading Kurt Schendel's affidavit.

'I have to have conclusive proof,' he said. Then, tapping the document with his finger: 'Now this is the sort of thing I was talking about. If Dr Schendel's informer – the man who actually heard what Barbie said – can be produced, and if he confirms what Barbie is reported to have said, then I promise you I will reopen the case.'

Beate's heart leaped. It was an important moment. 'Will you put that in writing?' she asked, pressing home her advantage.

'My secretary has gone home for the day.'

'That,' replied Beate, 'is no problem. I used to be a steno-grapher.'

She wound sheets of paper and carbon paper into a type-writer and took dictation from Ludolph.

Dear Mme Benguigi,

As a result of our talk today, I assure you that the material sent to me on 13 September by the French dele-gation, Mme Klarsfeld and yourself, will be carefully studied. As to Dr Schendel's affidavit of 8 September, it seems to me necessary to locate the witness who told Dr Schendel that the defendant said: 'Shot or deported — there is no difference.' If he can be found and will swear to that statement, I will be ready to reopen the prosecu-tion, for that will be proof that the defendant must at least have expected that his Jewish victims would be put to death.

In triumph the two women left the courthouse, distributing copies of Ludolph's letter to the knot of waiting newsmen as an insurance that the prosecutor would not undergo a further change of mind.

Soon afterwards Serge's painstaking tracing of all the sur-vivors of UGIF meeting in Paris turned up the man they wanted — Raymond Geissman, an appeal court lawyer, who clearly recalled the conversation with Barbie during which the fateful remark was made. He immediately dictated an affidavit to his secretary, part of which read:

Whenever I recall those anxious days thirty years ago, I remember that all of us were utterly convinced that the butchers on whom the life or death of our co-religionists depended knew perfectly well the terrible fate that awaited the people they had arrested.

I remember seeing Barbie 'frothing at the mouth' as he vented his hatred of the Jews, and his remark — 'Shot or deported — there is no difference' — was truly spoken by him. He said it in front of me and I reported it to my colleagues in Paris.

On 1 October, Beate returned to Munich and personally handed Ludolph a copy of the damning statement. Though the urbane lawyer made no secret of the fact that his personal opinion was that, after all the years 'the page ought to be turned', he kept his earlier promise and dictated an immediate official decision to his secretary:

SUBJECT: Public prosecutor's penal investigation in the Augsburg *Landesgericht* of Klaus Barbie for alleged complicity in murder.
1. The investigation will be reopened as to the charge against the defendant that he took part in the murder of French citizens of Jewish birth by deporting them to the east.
2. The decision for reopening the entire investigation will be delayed, but is hereby declared without prejudice.

Although Ludolph's earlier decision to support Rabl's recommendation that the case be shelved had modified to only qualified support for the Klarsfelds' campaign, he soon underwent a rapid sea-change and began to lobby vigorously on their behalf. Though Brandt's new protocol was still awaiting the Bundestag's ratification, he did all he could to bulldoze the case through and proved to be a valuable ally.

To the Nazi hunters he handed over two photographs, full-face and profile, taken of Barbie in 1943. To those he added a snapshot of a group of businessmen sitting round a table, one of whom bore a striking resemblance to the Butcher.

'The picture of the group,' he told them, 'was taken in La Paz, Bolivia, in 1968. That is all I can say at this time. Since you have demonstrated how efficient you are, why don't you help me identify that man?'

Anthropometrics is the science of identifying the tiny facial 'signatures', as unique to each person as his fingerprints, that make up the human physiognomy and which remain unchanged by the years or by disguise. Typically brazen, Beate marched into the office of the head of the French government's anthropometric department, waving aside questions as to whether Madame had an appointment, and badgered the expert into taking a look at her photographs. Protesting that the study would only be superficial and that he would not commit his opinion to paper, he nonetheless spent half an hour comparing the pictures before cautiously pronouncing that Barbie and the man on the shot from La Paz were, in all probability, one and the same. 'Look at the ears,' he said. 'His earlobes are turned outwards, particularly the right one, and that is unusual. The structure of the frontal bone on the left is common in all three pictures, and the folds at the corner of the mouth are absolutely identical.'

Ludolph was as excited by the news as the Klarsfelds. He promptly invited Beate to return to Munich at public expense for further consultations on the next moves in the pursuit of Barbie. Her new role as Ludolph's unofficial assistant amused her; she relished the paradox that she was still on bail from the Cologne court, awaiting trial for the attempted kidnapping of Kurt Lischka!

It was only a matter of time before the Klarsfelds' digging turned up the assumed name under which the fugitive was living – Klaus Altmann. It was a name which had been familiar to the West German government ever since 1969 when a secret report had been filed from their embassy in La Paz to the Foreign Office in Bonn. After chronicling Barbie's early days in Bolivia it went on:

Our investigations could not go much further, for Altmann enjoys extremely cordial relations with the Bolivian authorities. According to unconfirmed rumours, the Barbie family entered Bolivia with foreign [Vatican] passports. His daughter Ute asked us for a residence visa to the Federal Republic to work for the Böhringer Company[1] in Mannheim, which her father represents. She gave her father's previous nationality as Polish.

We advise you to make a very discreet inquiry for Klaus Altmann is very close to persons in the inner circle of the Bolivian government and to former Nazis now living in South America, such as Fritz Schwend[2] in Lima.

The Klarsfelds now had Barbie's assumed name and his photograph. All they needed was an address. On 28 December, 1971 they got it through contacts in Munich and Lima: Klaus Altmann, c/o Fritz Schwend, Santa Clara (via Lima), Casilla No. 1, Carretera Central.

Barbie had slipped over the border when news had reached him that Beate's campaign had finally stirred the Munich prosecutor's office into action. Her plan had been to pursue him in La Paz. Now she changed it and began making arrangements to fly to Lima, a trip that was to be paid for by a Jewish organisation of former Nazi deportees.

All she needed was documentary proof to take with her so that she could publicly demonstrate in the Peruvian capital that Altmann was Barbie. Here Manfred Ludolph came to her aid. On Tuesday, 26 January, 1972, the day before she was due to fly to Lima, she caught a plane to Munich and spent nine hours at the prosecutor's house compiling a report establishing 'Altmann's' identity. This, signed by the Munich attorney general, contained four essential proofs:

1. Klaus Altmann's daughter was born on 30 June, 1941 in Kassel, yet the register office had no such record. On the

[1] This was the firm to which Barbie sold his supplies of bark for the manufacture of quinine.
[2] Schwend, then a CIA agent in Peru, had been a wartime member of the RHSA, Berlin, from where he had masterminded the giant Nazi plot to ruin Britain's economy by flooding the international money market with forged five-pound notes.

other hand, Ute Barbie, daughter of Klaus Barbie, was registered as having been born at Trier on 30 June, 1941.

2. Klaus Altmann's son, Klaus-Georg, was said to have been born at Kasel, near Leipzig, on 11 December 1946. No such place exists, but on the same date Klaus-Jörg Barbie, son of Klaus, had been born at Kassel, a town 150 miles west of Leipzig.

3. Klaus Altmann's wife was named Regina and her maiden name was listed as Wilhelms. The maiden name of Barbie's wife was Regina Willms.

4. The anthropometrical examination of Professor Ziegel-mayer of the Ethnographical Institute of Munich University [commissioned by Ludolph after Beate's cornering of the French expert] showed that Barbie and Altmann were the same man.

News of Beate's impending visit to Lima stirred a hornets' nest in Peruvian government circles. In the early hours of 26 January, the day before her flight, Barbie was arrested and told he must return to Bolivia. He refused Peru's offer of a plane ticket as he did not want to leave his Volkswagen behind and, as a compromise, offered to drive back to Bolivia. The offer was accepted. On the day of Beate's flight, he bade farewell to Schwend and pointed his car towards the border, a two-day drive during which he had a constant police escort.

Beate arrived early next morning and immediately began an exhausting round of press conferences and, as Barbie raced for the border, hawked round the police and the presidential palace her documentary proof, signed by Munich's attorney general, that Altmann and Barbie were the same person. She begged that he be stopped before he reached the Bolivian border and slipped out of Peruvian jurisdiction.

At last she got action. A colonel in the Peruvian Intelligence Bureau rang the border to ask if the Volkswagen – licence number HH CD 360, registered in Hamburg in Klaus-Georg's name – has crossed into Bolivia. The answer was no. But in the end, Beate lost the race against the clock. In the last town before reaching the border, Barbie's police escort was handed a telegram stating that the German's expulsion order had been cancelled and that he could remain in Peru. Barbie, wisely, declined the offer and pressed on towards the border.

Beate rushed to the French embassy in the hope that diplomatic pressure from the ambassador, Albert Chambon, might close the border. But Chambon, though himself a former deportee and sympathetic to her cause, was still awaiting instructions from the Quai d'Orsay when news came through that Barbie had crossed into Bolivia. Once more the German was saved by political expediency; at the time France was more concerned with re-establishing ties with Peru after a series of protests from Lima about French atomic tests in the Pacific than in chasing an ageing war criminal.

By shuttling the problem back to Bolivia, France and Peru were left free to continue their diplomatic negotiations with a clear conscience. Beate, whose view was less pragmatic, announced her intention of going on to La Paz to continue hounding the Butcher. She booked a seat on the next flight across the Andes.

Her arrival at the capital's airport was received coolly by Bolivian officials. Three plainclothes detectives relieved her of her passport and recommended that she install herself in the Hôtel Sucre. There she held another round of press conferences ('The reporters came into my room while others waited in the corridor. I might as well have had a red light outside my door.') before, ever the quintessential woman, seeking out a hairdresser. As a precaution, she changed her room at the Sucre; the ground-floor one she had been given on checking in was too handy for a passer-by who might feel inclined to loose a couple of shots through the window or lob in a bomb.

Beate's reception by the French embassy in La Paz was correct but unhelpful. 'The ambassador is not in,' was the response to her numerous requests for an interview. Her attempts to reach someone sufficiently Olympian in the Bolivian Interior Ministry were even more disheartening. 'Mañana,' was the answer she received each time from the armed guard outside.

On Wednesday, 2 February, three days after her arrival in La Paz, Beate was expelled for contravening Bolivian visa and tourist regulations. But by then she did not care. On orders from Paris the French ambassador had formally demanded Barbie's extradition and the ex-Gestapo chief's name was prominent in headlines all over the world. Without demur she collected her confiscated passport and, flying via Lima, returned home.

Four days later – on 6 February – Banzer's police arrested Barbie on a tax-dodge charge but he was quickly released. Ironically he discharged part of his debt with money he had earned from granting an interview to French television. Back home in Paris, Beate set about raising funds from well-wishers to pay for another trip to La Paz; this time she was determined to keep the pot boiling with a newsworthy stunt that would ensure that the Barbie affair remained a running story. She invited Itta Halaunbrenner to accompany her. Despite her age and the altitude of the Bolivian capital – 13,000 feet above sea level – Mme Halaunbrenner immediately agreed to make the trip. She told me eleven years later:

> I would have agreed to anything that would stir public opinion against that man. The thought of him living a comfortable life when my children were no more than ashes cut me like a knife. If Beate Klarsfeld had asked me to fly to the moon, I would have gone with her willingly.

The two women flew from Paris on Sunday, 20 February and stopped off for a day in Lima in order to maximise their press coverage with a series of interviews with newsmen. Their stay in the Peruvian capital was prolonged while the

Bolivian government dithered over entry visas, but finally, on Wednesday, 23 February news came that President Banzer himself had granted them permission to land in the country.

Next day they flew to La Paz, arriving at 12.30 p.m., and they had not even left the aircraft before a young government official climbed aboard asking for Señora Klarsfeld. He extracted from her a promise that she would make no statements to the newspapers. If she did, he warned, she would be expelled from the country at once. Lying through her teeth, Beate gave her word.

From officials she heard information that was disheartening. There were to be no extradition proceedings against Barbie. 'President Banzer thinks he has enough evidence to consider the problem settled,' said the presidential spokesman, Alfredo Arce.

And Barbie's lawyer announced: 'Bolivia is an inviolable asylum, and all who take refuge in it are sacrosanct. The time limit for the prosecution of major crimes in Bolivia is eight years. Altmann-Barbie's are, therefore, ancient history. The petty deception that Barbie practised by disguising himself as Altmann is, at the most, punishable by a small fine.'

The following day, Friday, Beate and Itta were granted an interview with Jaime Tapia, the deputy foreign minister, who clucked sympathetically and patted Itta on the shoulder when she wept as she recounted the tragic story of her children's deaths. But it became apparent that the sympathy was not going to be backed by any action.

Having followed the law so far by furnishing the proper authorities with the Barbie data – to no good effect – Beate set out to break the promise she had made on arrival at La Paz airport. On Monday, 28 February, from her room at La Paz Hotel, she began telephoning newsmen, inviting them to a press conference at 11 a.m. that morning. It was short notice but she feared that if she picked a later time the news would leak out and the police step in to prevent her from speaking. She had underestimated the power of the Bolivian police over the Press. Three-quarters of an hour before the start of the conference, half a dozen plain clothes men entered the lobby of the hotel and asked Beate to accompany them to headquarters.

She went to her room to pick up her coat and found two more policemen on guard outside her door. In a jeep she was driven to the office of Major Dito Vargas, head of the Bolivian secret service, who warned her solemnly, through an interpreter, against holding a press conference. If she did, she would be expelled.

The jeep dropped her back at the hotel at 10.50. Ten minutes later she began the conference and Itta once more told her anguished story. She finished talking at 12.15 p.m., just as two policemen returned and hustled Beate down to headquarters once more. There she was locked up and left to cool her heels until 5 p.m. when Hermán Arteaga, head of the *Policia Internacional*, entered and bluntly told her to keep her mouth shut in future. 'This is your last warning,' he said. 'Next time you will be arrested.'

Tuesday morning's newspapers had a field day retailing the press conference information, with whole pages devoted to the bloody career of Altmann-Barbie and the horrors of the Nazi concentration camps. When the two women left the hotel they were surrounded by well-wishers. 'We are with you,' they were told. 'Our country should chuck Barbie out to pay for his crimes.'

That morning Beate was arrested again and made the by-then familiar journey to police HQ. A story went out on the agency wires that she had been taken away by two men who had not been identified as police officers, causing alarm in France until the Bolivian government, sensing a rumpus, invited a journalist from Reuters to visit Beate to confirm that she had not been kidnapped. Soon afterwards a police superintendent who spoke a little French tried to question Beate, but was so bombarded with indignant questions from her about why she was being held that he lost his temper and shouted: 'You shit on us, so we're going to shit on you and kick your arse out of here.' That evening she was released and allowed to rejoin Itta at La Paz Hotel.

Throughout her time in La Paz, Beate had been badgering the French ambassador, Jean-Louis Mandereau, to press the Bolivians more firmly into action against Barbie. Finally, at her instigation (and probably in the hope of getting this remarkably wilful young woman out of his hair) His Excellency made a formal application for a confrontation between Itta Halaunbrenner and the man who had robbed her of her children. As might be expected, the Butcher refused the invitation.

Beate herself did and does not have the least interest in meeting Barbie or, indeed any of the Nazis she has tracked down. It seems strange but she is totally incurious about them. I suspect she fears meeting them in case her iron resolve wavers when her monsters turn out to have human faces. The tubby old man in La Paz was not the Barbie she sought; her prey was the young, vigorous Barbie of thirty years earlier.

With confrontation out of the question some new way had to be found of keeping the affair on the boil, so the two women decided to take recourse to legal action with Mme Halaunbrenner suing as an individual for the murder of four of her family. The first lawyer they approached turned the case down for political reasons; the second demanded a fee of $7,000, an impossibly high figure that was clearly designed to deter them from issuing proceedings.

A caustic Beate announced at a press conference: 'Bolivian justice is too expensive for us.' Wickedly she then trotted out an old Bolivian proverb: 'Beware of Chilean women, Peruvian friends, and Bolivian justice.'

On the morning of Monday, 6 March she prepared to leave La Paz with Itta, procuring an exit visa from the Ministry of the Interior, getting the passports in order and booking seats on the 8 p.m. flight to Lima. The men at the ministry must have breathed deep sighs of relief at the pro-

spect of ridding themselves at last of this stubborn and tur-
bulent redhead – but she had one more surprise in store for
them.

Around noon she and Itta strolled through the chill air of
La Paz to the Prado, the capital's busiest street, in which the
headquarters of Transmaritima were situated. With them
they had lengths of chain and padlocks, bought especially
the day before, and two placards written in Spanish.
Opposite the shipping line's office, they chained themselves
to a bench and held up their placards. Itta's which carried a
picture of her dead family, read: *Listen Bolivians! As a
mother I claim only justice. I want Barbie-Altmann, who
murdered my husband and three of my children, brought to
trial.* Beate's read: *In the name of millions of Nazi victims,
let Barbie-Altmann be extradited.*

A large crowd quickly gathered and cars on the Prado
ground to a halt in a tangled traffic jam. The bystanders
were sympathetic. One woman called out: 'There is no such
thing as justice in Bolivia! Kidnap him or kill him.' Later a
police jeep arrived; its occupants read the placards, then
drove off. At 4 p.m. a small truck drew up, disgorging a
handful of plainclothes men who mingled with the watchers
before, at a given signal, leaping forward, snatching the
placards and taking to their heels. Some members of the
knot of sympathisers, amongst them an Israeli tourist,
fashioned new signs within a few minutes. Then the Press
arrived and a reporter held out a microphone to Beate,
asking what the chains signified.

'They are the chains that bind Bolivia to Nazism,' she
replied.

A member of the French embassy who was passing in
front of her, surveying the protest with disapproval, said
frostily: 'What you are doing won't accomplish anything.'

He was wrong. The formidable spitfire and the courageous Mme Halaunbrenner had pitchforked Barbie back
into the world's headlines. The French were once again
pressing for extradition and the Bolivian government was

increasingly on the defensive.

A year after the two women flew out of La Paz on the flight to Lima, the Gestapo man was taken into 'protective custody' in San Pedro prison. By then Beate had called a temporary halt to her Nazi-hunting activities in order to give birth to her second child, her daughter, Lida, but took comfort from the fact that her adversary was, at last, getting a taste of prison life.

One day, she vowed, he would be in a cell for the rest of his life.

There was a chilling postscript to the La Paz visit. Back in Paris Beate had accepted an invitation to address a meeting in Cannes and had taken her son, Arno, with her. They left on 10 May. Serge remained at home, his mother, Raissa, staying with him.

At 5 p.m. the concierge delivered a parcel, addressed to Mme Klarsfeld, which had been left with her. Raissa took charge of it, noting that the sender's address did not coincide with the postmark. An hour and a half later, Serge arrived home and removed the outer wrapping, revealing a soft cardboard box. Inside that, wrapped in tissue, was a second box done up in fancy paper and bearing the name of a well-known confectionery. It contained a cylindrical box labelled 'Sugar'.

Suspiciously Serge put a speck of the contents, a powder with black flecks, on his tongue. It tasted sour. A few scraps of the powder had fallen into the sink and he put a match to them. They immediately burst into flames. Carefully he packed the boxes and contents into a shopping bag and took them to Auteuil police station. 'I think this might be a bomb.' he said. The duty officer hastily called the fire department and asked them to send a bomb disposal expert. Cautiously he cut into the package. Inside were enough explosives and six-inch nails to blow an unwary opener to bits.

EPILOGUE

The last chapter in the extraordinary saga of Klaus Barbie remains to be told, yet it lies tantalisingly hidden over the horizon. More than a year has elapsed since the gates of Montluc closed behind him, yet there is still no sign that the irritable Christian Riss, the overworked examining magistrate of Lyon, is any closer to the day when he will have Barbie standing in the dock before him.

Justice has been a long time coming to the ageing Rhinelander. Twice France found him guilty and sentenced him to death. That punishment cannot now be meted out for one of President Mitterrand's first acts after his election victory was to abolish the death penalty. Nor can Barbie be charged with the war crimes for which he has already been convicted ... nor, indeed, with any war crimes because they, like all serious crimes in France, carry a statute of limitations of twenty years, after which time, the criminal is free of any risk of prosecution.

That leaves 'crimes against humanity' as the only possible charge since no time limit applies to them. But how do you define a crime against humanity? This type of charge originated from some hasty legal cobbling by Allied lawyers tasked with building a case against the leaders of the Nazi regime at the Nuremberg trials.

Such a charge seemed the only means of arraigning the Nazi hierarchy for atrocities which, at the time of their commission, were perfectly legal under Third Reich law. Their acts were declared retrospecitvely illegal and those found guilty were hanged or imprisoned. That those sentences were justly deserved there can be no doubt, but the creation of retrospective laws offends against the very fundamentals of justice. It is surely a case of desirable ends being used to justify dubious means – a concept not unfamiliar to the Nazis' own creed.

Yet without 'crimes against humanity' or something similar, the Nazi leaders would have been untouchable. So the legal draughtsmen did their work, came up with the improvisation of 'crimes against humanity' and incorporated it into the Nuremberg Charter. The definition in the Charter reads as follows:

> Murder, extermination, deportation and other inhumane acts committed against any civilian population, before or during the war, or persecution on political, racial or religious grounds in execution of, or in connection with, any crimes within the jurisdiction of the Tribunal, whether or not in violation of the domestic law of the country where perpetrated.

It was a clumsy law, hard to define and open to almost any interpretation, but it served its purpose of making the Nazi leaders answerable for their actions. It was, however, never intended for use against individual German soldiers operating in the field; crimes committed by them were amply covered by long-established rules of war and the Geneva Convention. At the end of the war none of the Allies incorporated crimes against humanity into their domestic penal codes. None, that is, until France, realising in 1964 that the twenty-year statute of limitations would put Nazi war criminals beyond reach of the law, quickly embraced the Nuremberg concept, tacked it on to her domestic penal code and declared it exempt from any statute of limitations.

Barbie's lawyers will no doubt argue long and hard that his actions in Lyon and Haute-Savoie were not crimes against humanity; that he was only the third-ranking Gestapo officer in the city, and therefore not responsible for general orders; that he was not at Izieu and did not know

the ultimate destination of the children or any other deportees; that the telexes he sent relating to Izieu were purely
an administrative task which fell to him.

Serge Klarsfeld, who will speak at the trial on behalf of
Barbie's Jewish victims, dismisses such defence arguments
out of hand:

> It is because of the children of Izieu that Barbie will be
> convicted. Many children's homes like that one existed in
> France in those days and every Gestapo officer in the
> country except two chose to ignore them and leave then
> unmolested. One was Alois Brunner; the other was
> Barbie.
>
> As for his claim that he did not know what fate awaited
> the deportees, well, we have his own words on the subject:
> 'Shot or deported – there is no difference.'
>
> And who dares say that the slaughter of those innocent
> children was not a crime against humanity?

Barbie's lawyer, the hard-line Marxist Jacques Verges, is
also preparing a vigorous challenge of the means that were
used to oust his client from Bolivia, saying that the use of a
disguised French Hercules to move the expelled man was an
illegal act, connived at by the Bolivian and French govern-
ments. It is certainly a valid legal argument, but it would be
indeed a single-minded judge who would set Barbie free on
those grounds. But for the incredible, behind-the-scenes
wrangling between La Paz, Lima, Paris and Bonn, President
Zuazo might have got his wish of a totally legal extradition.
Instead he got something else. Within weeks of Barbie's
return to France, the French government signed an agreement to deliver twelve Mirage warplanes to the Bolivian Air
Force.

Inevitably Barbie's reappearance in Lyon has opened many
old wounds and the media disclosures that have followed
that reappearance have turned up many revealing stones.

One of the most significant has been a rediscovered report
from Ernst Kaltenbrunner, head of the RSHA, to Foreign
Minster von Ribbentrop, dated 29 June 1943, eight days
after Barbie's coup at Caluire. It was headed: 'Concerning
the "Secret Army" in France', and begins:

> Measures taken to destroy the leadership of the Secret
> Army have so far had the following results.
>
> In a letter box, which the *Einsatzkommando* of the
> Security Police and the SS in Lyon know to be that of the
> chief of the railway sabotage department of the 3rd
> section of the Secret Army, whose cover names are known
> to be 'Didot' and 'Bardot', were found several letters
> which had been sent to him by the central bureau of the
> United Resistance Movements. Among others was a com-
> munication dated 27 May 1943, according to which
> 'Didot' was expected at 9 a.m. on 9 June 1943, at the
> Muette métro station where he would meet the General.
>
> 'Didot' was, in fact, the railway engineer and lieu-
> tenant in the Reserves, René Louis Hardy.
>
> By keeping the appointment at the Muette station our-
> selves, we were able to arrest the General after he re-
> sponded to the password 'Didot'. He was Charles George
> Antoine Delestraint. . . . After an uninterrupted interro-
> gation lasting fifty hours, General Delestraint admitted to
> being chief of the Secret Army with the cover name
> 'Vidal' and that he had been promoted by de Gaulle.

The report went on:

> During the course of interrogation, the chief of railway
> sabotage Hardy, alias 'Didot', made a full statement and
> admitted, among other things, to having developed a plan
> of about 150 pages on operations for the sabotage of the
> railways to be realised in the event of an Anglo–American
> invasion which he had submitted to his superior for
> scrutiny. His closest collaborator in the area of railway

sabotage was the Jew, Heilbronner, alias, 'Arel', alias 'Hennequin' who, thanks to Hardy's help, was arrested at a rendezvous.

Hardy, thanks to his ample statements and his willingness to collaborate, was able to be used successfully several times at rendezvous. Furthermore, he was able to reveal from memory the plan of railway sabotage for the benefit of the German Services.

Of the meeting at Caluire, Kaltenbrunner reported the arrest of six men and went on:

The meeting had been called by the chief of 'Mouvements Unis de Resistance' who had been appointed by General de Gaulle and who used the cover name 'Max'

'Max' himself did not go to the meeting. He had probably been detained in a raid by the French police.

The Kaltenbrunner report came as a bombshell when it was published in *Paris Match* in March 1983.

Its existence has been known for years. Indeed, references were made to it during Hardy's second trial in 1950, though the extracts offered in evidence were little more than generalised resumés, incomplete and lacking in detail. The tribunal did not recognise their importance and ended with a hung verdict. But it would be wrong, even now, to jump to conclusions. In the twilight world of espionage anything and everything is possible.

Of the Klarsfelds, only Serge still maintains an interest in the Barbie case, for it is he who must represent the interests of so many of the Butcher's Jewish victims when the old German finally comes to trial. Beate, typically, has shown no interest since he arrived back in Lyon. He is a man of the past who, one day, will be called to explain his wrongs of the past.

She, still only 45, is a woman of today seeking accused

men for tomorrow's war-crimes trials. She lives in constant danger of her life for the bonds of the *Odessa* and *Kamaradenschaft* still hold together the brotherhood of the SS. Death threats are a constant worry and she fears always for the safety of her children, Arno, now 18, and Lida, 11. In 1979 a timebomb planted in the family car in their apartment block parking space, blew the vehicle to pieces and damaged twenty others. Mercifully no one was hurt.

Beate has been showered with awards and honours by the Jewish world and, in 1977, became the first non-Jewish German to be nominated by Israel for the Nobel Peace Prize.

She has been arrested, imprisoned, assaulted, spat on and villified. She has been accused of being a Zionist, a Marxist, and a Communist. Somehow, in all this whirl of political activity, she manages to remain an elegant, middle-class Parisian housewife whose beautifully furnished apartment is immaculate. Even when she is on the trail of some elderly Nazi, it is the thought of her home and family which sustains her: 'I try to concentrate on the important things of life: Did I leave Arno enough clean underwear? Will Serge remember to shine his shoes? Or, disaster of disasters, will he know to look for the laundry ticket under the TV set, otherwise he'll have no clean clothes?'

At the time of writing, (February 1984), Beate Klarsfeld is away from home on yet another crusade, potentially her most dangerous yet. On 10 February she arrived in Asunción, the capital of Paraguay, to launch a campaign against the most notorious Nazi killer still alive – Dr Josef Mengele, the 'Angel of Death'. Many people have tried to find Mengele; several have never returned – they have joined the estimated 400,000 victims of his who died in Auschwitz.

Klaus Barbie remains the enigma of this story – the polite and amusing charmer who could kill in black rage or in cold blood – the devoted husband who was able to look on as his pet Alsatian savaged the bodies of his female suspects – the loving father who would force the fingers of a young Resist-

ance worker into a door hinge and repeatedly slam the door
shut until the digits were reduced to mangled stumps.

The miserable career of this small, undistinguished-
looking German has touched, scarred and fouled the lives of
many thousands of people from two continents, bringing
them pain, dread and death. The grief he has created is in-
calculable. Throughout the span of my lifetime (I was born
four days after his daughter, Ute), he has killed, maimed and
corrupted. That is a long innings. The price he will pay — a
few years in prison and a peaceful death in his cell — seems
remarkably cheap.

During both world wars British soldiers used two words to
describe the Germans. One was 'Jerries', an almost affec-
tionate name implying respect for the ordinary soldiers they
faced in battle; the other was 'Huns', directed at those of the
enemy whose ruthless disregard for the rules of war put
them beyond the pale. Applied to Klaus Barbie, the term is
not pejorative, for the Oxford Dictionary defines it as 'a
reckless destroyer'.

Like Attila, the scourge of God, Barbie is a Hun.

In the summer of 1983 I was in a Munich *Bierkeller*
where the air was smoky and busty *Fraüleins* weaved
through the swaying, singing crowds carrying armfuls of
brimming beer glasses while leather-clad Tyrolean-hatted
musicians sweated their way through a series of jaunty
waltzes. This Bavarian capital was where it all began more
than half a century earlier; here in a *Bierkeller* just like the
one I was in, Hitler had dreamed his dreams of a new order.

The band ended their waltz with a flourish and put down
their instruments to tackle the huge *Steins* of beer which the
waitress had ferried to them from the bar. The roar of conversation and laughter rose to fill the void caused by the
temporary absence of music. When they had drunk their fill
the bandsmen reclaimed their instruments. A staccato drum
roll suddenly silenced the crowd and ushered in the triumphant blare of brass and the clear, ringing notes of the

glockenspiel. At the heart of the insistent rhythm of the flamboyant march was the big drum, thudding to the traditional soldier's pace of 120 steps a minute.

Yells of approval turned into the words of the song that accompanied the march. Beer glasses thumped on to table-tops in time with the music, feet stamped up and down on the floor like those of troops marking time on a parade square. It was stirring, and faintly disturbing, to see how instantly this pack of good-natured Bavarian drinkers could be gripped and led into these bawling swaggerings.

Next day I went to Dachau.

The place is a neat, inoffensive-looking township, just off the autobahn on Munich's north-west fringes. You pass a busy garden centre, its lawn strewn with wickerwork furniture for sale, and glimpse with a shock of recognition, the watch towers and the barbed wire that, until then, you have seen only in scratchy old newsreels. Beside the camp is a large car park. As my companion, Ciaran Donnelly, doubling as interpreter and photographer, and I walked past the vehicles towards the camp entrance, a glossy coach set down a party of German students, teenage boys and girls. Like all youngsters freed from the classroom for the day they were in a happy mood, laughing and calling to each other as they made their way through the car park. Young, blonde Germans, smiling and full of fun; Germans of a different epoch to those who had created the grim place towards which Donnelly and I were heading.

The filthy, lice-ridden huts that once marched in twin rows down the centre of the concentration camp have long gone, razed to rid them of their vermin, their stink and their memories. Just two remain as reminders, gaunt blocks filled with scarred wooden tiers, like the shelves of a left-luggage office, which served as the cramped beds of thousands.

Across the compound, set into the guardhouse, are the original iron gates to which the railway lines led and through which so many men, women and children marched into hell. Incorporated in the ironwork is the motto *Arbeit*

Macht Frei ('Work makes you free'). Only death freed most of the inmates from Dachau.

Their corpses were burned in the crematorium which stands amid trim privet hedges at the far end of the camp. Donnelly and I tramped past the ovens with their yawning doors, through the morgue and into the gas chamber. This one, the guidebook informed us, had never been used but was the prototype for others which functioned so admirably in other camps. It was a largish, oblong room, clinically tiled and dimly lit. Drain grates studded the floors and mock shower heads sprouted from the ceiling. I began to remember Edith Klebinder telling me how the children died first. . . . A few minutes later we saw the young Germans who had arrived with us. The laughter and the horseplay were gone. Their healthy faces were grey with anguish. Most sat with their heads in their hands, others with their eyes fixed on some invisible spot. One strapping youth of about 18 wept incontrollably, his girlfriend ignoring her own tears as she tried to comfort him.

Appendix A

SS Ranks and their equivalents

SS	British Army	US Army
Reichsführer-SS	Field-Marshal	General of the Army
SS-*Oberstgruppenführer*	General	General
SS-*Obergruppenführer*	Lieutenant-General	Lieutenant-General
SS-*Gruppenführer*	Major-General	Major-General
SS-*Brigadeführer*	Brigadier	Brigadier-General
SS-*Oberführer*	—	—
SS-*Standartenführer*	Colonel	Colonel
SS-*Obersturmbannführer*	Lieutenant-Colonel	Lieutenant-Colonel
SS-*Sturmbannführer*	Major	Major
SS-*Hauptsturmführer*	Captain	Captain
SS-*Obersturmführer*	Lieutenant	Lieutenant
SS-*Untersturmführer*	Second Lieutenant	Second Lieutenant
SS-*Sturmscharführer*	Regimental Sergeant-Major	Sergeant-Major
SS-*Hauptscharführer*	Sergeant-Major	Master-Sergeant
SS-*Oberscharführer*	Quartermaster-Sergeant	Technical Sergeant
SS-*Scharführer*	Staff Sergeant	Staff Sergeant
SS-*Unterscharführer*	Sergeant	Sergeant
SS-*Rottenführer*	Corporal	Corporal
SS-*Sturmmann*	Lance Corporal	
SS-*Oberschütze*	—	Private 1st Class
SS-*Schütze*	Private	Private

Appendix B
Glossary

Abwehr	Intelligence and Clandestine Warfare Service of the German High Command
Amt	An office, branch or directorate of a ministry
Ausweis	Pass or travel permit
BEF	British Expeditionary Force
CDJC	Centre de Documentation Juive et Contemporaine – Jewish Contemporary Documentation Centre, Paris
CDU	Christian Democratic Union – West Germany's largest Conservative party
CGQJ	Commissariat Général aux Questions Juives – department of the Vichy government dealing with Jewish affairs
CIA	US Central Intelligence Agency
CIC	US Counter Intelligence Corps
CNR	Conseil National de la Résistance – national council of Resistance leaders founded by Jean Moulin
CROWCASS	Central Registry of War Criminals and Security Suspects
DAD	US Department of Army Detachment – organisation of non-military espionage teams operating in post-war Germany under military cover
Didot	Cover name for René Hardy, head of Résistance Fer
Drancy	Holding camp in Paris from which deportees were transported East
Einsatzgruppe	Task force of the Sipo and SD for special missions (usually liquidations) in Occupied territory and consisting of up to six

	Einsatzkommandos
Einsatzkommando	Detachment of the Sipo; part of an *Einsatzgruppe*
Führer	Leader
Gestapo	*Geheime Staatspolizei* – Secret State Police
Kamaradenschaft	Network of former SS men pledged to keep alive Nazi ideals
KGB	Russian Secret Service
Kommandatur	A German military headquarters
Kripo	*Kriminalpolizei* which together with the Gestapo formed the Security Police (Sipo)
Luftwaffe	German Air Force
Max	Cover name for Jean Moulin who also used the named 'Rex', 'Regis' and 'Martel'
Milice	French collaborationist militia
MI5	British Military Intelligence (internal)
MI6	British Military Intelligence (overseas)
MI9	British Military Intelligence department organising escape routes out of Occupied Europe
MIS	US Military Intelligence Service
NKVD	Former name of KGB
NSB	Dutch Nazi Party
NSDAP	Nationalsozialistische Deutsche Arbeiter Partei – The Nazi Party
Odessa	Organisation der Ehemalingen SS-Angehörigen – Organisation of former SS members
OFA	Franco-German Alliance for Youth
OPC	Office of Policy Co-ordination – a branch of the US State Department
Panzer	German tank
Popular Front	Anti-Franco forces during the Spanish Civil War
Reich	The German empire
Reichstag	The German parliament
Résistance Fer	Railway sabotage group headed by René Hardy
Rijkinstituut voor Oorlogsdocumentatie	Dutch War Documentation Institute, Amsterdam

RSHA	*Reichssicherheitshauptamt* – Reich Central Security Department formed in 1939 and combining the Security Police (Gestapo and Kripo) and the SS Security Service (SD)
RuSHA	*Rasse-und Siedlungshauptamt* – SS Department for Race and Resettlement, concerned with the racial purity of the SS
SA	*Sturmabteilung* – literally 'Storm Detachment', the original Nazi paramilitary 'Brownshirts'
SD	*Sicherheitsdienst* – the SS Security Service
Sipo	Sicherheitzpolizei – Security Police
SNCF	Société National des Chemins de Fer – the French national railway system
SOE	Special Operations Executive – British liaison and support organisation to aid the French Resistance
Sonderkommando	Concentration camp prioners detailed to man the gas chambers and crematoria
SS	*Schutzstaffel* – literally 'Guard Detachment'
Statut des Juifs	Statute on the Jews – anti-Semitic laws passed by Vichy France
Sureté	French Criminal Investigation Department
UGIF	Union Générale des Israélites de France – organisation formed by the Germans to liaise between the Occupying forces and France's Jewish community
Vidal	Cover name for General Delestraint, head of the Secret Army
Volksturm	Literally 'People's Storm' – a last-ditch civil defence organisation which pressed old men and young boys into military service
Waffen-SS	Fully militarised SS formation
Wehrmacht	German armed forces
Zyklon-B	Hydrate of cyanide used in the gas chambers of the death camps

Bibliography

Aron, Robert, *De Gaulle Triumphant* (Putnam, New York)

Bower, Tom, *Klaus Barbie, Butcher of Lyons* (Michael Joseph, London)

Butler, Josephine, *Churchill's Secret Agent* (Blaketon-Hall, Exeter)

Foot, M.R.D., *Six Faces of Courage* (Eyre Methuen, London)

Fuchs, Gottlieb, *Le Renard* (Editions Albin Michel, Paris)

Goldberg, Michel, *Namesake* (Yale University Press, Yale)

Goralski, Robert, *World War II Almanack* (Hamish Hamilton, London)

Harzer, Philippe, *Klaus Barbie et la Gestapo en France* (le Carousel-FN, Paris)

Höhne, Heinz, *The Order of the Death's Head* (Pan, London)

Klarsfeld, Beate, *Wherever They May Be* (Vanguard Press, New York)

Knight, Frida *The French Resistance* (Lawrence and Wishart, London)

Lengel, Olga, *Five Chimneys* (Granada, London)

Loftus, John, *The Belarus Secret* (Penguin, London)

Marrus, Michael R., and Paxton, Robert O., *Vichy France and the Jews* (Basic Books, New York)

Schoenbrun, David, *Soldiers of the Night* (Robert Hale, London)

INDEX